ON HISTORY'S COATTAILS

MICHAEL HENDERSON

Michael Henderson

GROSVENOR USA

Published by
Grosvenor USA
8503 Patterson Avenue, Suite 10
Richmond, VA 23229

Also available from
Grosvenor Books
54 Lyford Road
London SW18 3JJ
England

302, 141 Somerset Street West
Ottawa, Ontario, K2P 2H1
Canada

21 Dorcas Street
South Melbourne, Victoria 3205
Australia

PO Box 1834
Wellington
New Zealand

Library of Congress Card Number 88–081 477
British Library Cataloguing-in-Publication Data

Henderson, Michael Douglas
    On history's coattails: commentaries by
    an English journalist in America.
    1. World events, 1900–
    I. Title
    909.82

    ISBN 1–85239–503–6

Book design: Blair Cummock
Cover design: Bill Cameron-Johnson
Cover illustration: Fredrika Spillman

Typeset in 11pt Sabon by Input Typesetting Ltd.
Printed in the United States of America

TO ERICA

By the same author

FROM INDIA WITH HOPE

EXPERIMENT WITH UNTRUTH

A DIFFERENT ACCENT

Contents

1 A personal word   1

Forty years ago   2
A different accent   4
Mt. Hood 1   7
Mt. Hood 2   9
Beneath the jellyfish   12
Dad   14

2 Courage personified   19

Lock up the silver!   20
A yen to serve   22
Sullivan's principles   25
Buried alive   27
Unarmed among headhunters   29
A corpse looked back   32
What a great God   34

3   In a lighter vein   39

    An English revolution   40
    Encounters of a royal kind   43
    Old age is unexpected   45
    Polls apart   48
    Trickle-down theory   51
    What farmers know   53
    Travel travail   56

4   Peacemaking   59

    Peace at a fair price   60
    Patron saint of hostages   61
    Out of the present darkness   65
    A quiet night in Beirut   67
    After the killing fields   70
    Red repentance   72
    Don't curse the French   74
    Last words of an Irish lass   77

5   On my mind   81

    Useless Europeans   82
    Twelve steps   84
    Shooting the cabinet   87
    Holy gamble   90
    Christians kill Christ   92
    No punishment from God   95
    Good on'ya, mate   97
    Spiritual interdependence   99
    An honest coach   102

6   Americana   105

    My soul is a strange companion   106
    Not a spark of genius   108
    Sticking your neck out   111

Tongue in cheekbone 114
Kitchen help 117
Shipwrecked on purpose 119
A ten-gallon story 121
A proper Bostonian 124
Driving a hard bargain 126

7 Flying the flag 129

All but doomed 130
When the barriers rise 132
Fire engine for Africa 135
Left for dead 138
Prince Charles 140
Sharp practice 142
God's politician 145

8 Around the globe 149

Collision or collusion 150
Give us bad news 152
The unguarded Prime Minister 154
Indian Apartheid 157
Waiting to die 160
Christianity of obedience 163
Halos rust easily 166
When did you last steal? 168

9 Back to basics 173

Mass cheating 174
Setting a murderer free 177
Jack Anderson's discovery 179
Lasers of the spirit 182
Through enemy lines 184
A close shave 187
If the cap fits. . . . 190

1 A personal word

"I was brought to America by a drunken duchess – and other perspectives of a resident alien." This was a suggestion I gave my publisher as a title to this book. It was not thought appropriate.

But it is accurate. Just.

I *was* brought to the United States in 1940 by *The Duchess of York*. It was a class of ocean liners nicknamed "the drunken duchesses" because of their ungainly progress through water.

I *am* a resident alien.

Henry James wrote, "If it is good to have one foot in England, it is still better, or at least as good, to have the other out of it." I don't think I quite go along with the sentiment I hear behind those words. But having always kept one foot in England while the other was placed in some thirty or forty lands I *do* have other perspectives.

Many of those perspectives stem from association with the men and women of Moral Re-Armament, which in 1988–9 marks its 50th anniversary.

So this first chapter will tell you, as they say here, where I'm coming from.

2 A personal word
Forty years ago

FORTY YEARS ago this week I was very sick. Seasick. I was tossing about the mid-Atlantic on a little aircraft carrier, HMS *Patroller*, which was escorting a convoy headed for Britain. HMS *Patroller* was a converted American merchant ship, built in Seattle. We were topheavy because we were carrying a squadron of planes on deck as well as in the hangar. We were in a storm that had lasted a week and were zigzagging to avoid any German submarines that hadn't heard the war was over. As it happened a submarine surrendered to us, the German crew was taken aboard, and a skeleton British crew took the submarine to Canada. It was all very exciting for a thirteen-year-old.

I had spent five years as an English evacuee in the United States and was returning home to my parents and country. With last week's anniversary of VE Day, the ending of the war in Europe, many reminiscences have been shared, and so I thought I might add the perspective of someone who was very young at that time.

At the age of seven, in 1939, I remember being outfitted with a gas mask at school, watching tanks maneuver on the beach, counting bombers as they flew low over the house, being fascinated by barrage balloons. Then a year later, in August 1940, my brother and I were two of thousands of children sent for safety to the United States, Canada, and even as far as Australia and New Zealand. Some went privately and some under a plan set in motion just two months earlier by the British cabinet on the day France capitulated. There would have been more than 200,000, all those who had applied, but for the fact that in September 77 children drowned when their ship was sunk and the government refused to let any more go.

We sailed in what was then the largest convoy in history. Next to us was the battleship HMS *Revenge* and as far as you could see in every direction to the horizon there were ships. Ironically, I recall sitting on our bunks playing the latest game we had learned, Battleships, where the aim was to sink each other's warships. Our arrival in Boston is recorded for posterity with a photo on the front page of a morning paper. My brother has his tongue stuck out at the photographer.

There are many relatively unknown adventures from that period. For instance, on August 30 a ship carrying 320 children was torpedoed at night off the coast of Ireland. The children took to the lifeboats singing "There'll always be an England" and were subsequently rescued by other ships. However, inadvertently, one nine-year-old boy was left on board the ship which had been hit twice. He awoke, found the ship abandoned, and went back to sleep. The next morning he waved to a destroyer and was rescued.

In America we felt we did our bit for the war effort, spotting for planes, collecting scrap metal, growing vegetables, saving toward war bonds, cheering Churchill when he spoke at Harvard. I was even trusted with the lowering and raising of the American flag, and played a part in a school production about Nathan Hale. It is sad to recall now that a favorite board game at one point was called, I think, Target for Tonight, and consisted of throwing dice to advance on bomber raids over German cities. This was the time of sending "bundles for Britain," and my brother and I went to one fancy dress party as "bundles from Britain."

For five years an American family with whom we had had no connection looked after us as if we were their own. It was a wonderful demonstration of American hospitality and generosity. And returning to Britain we were enriched with many experiences and new perspectives. Our parents who had been totally involved in the war effort – our father in the general staff, our mother in the censorship – may have been a little irritated at our belief that America won the war. Our uncle, an artillery officer who had been shelled by his American allies, may have been a little jaundiced in his view of the Yanks. But the predominant thought of our family and of the whole nation forty years ago was one of great gratitude to America and the Americans and what they had done to help preserve liberty in the world.

Our wartime adventures may seem slight and our five-year separation from our parents a small price to pay when one considers the sufferings of others. But our gratitude was as great as anyone's and bears re-expressing today. It has certainly affected for good my attitude toward Americans ever since.

May 16, 1985

A different accent

MY WIFE Erica, who is English too, made a long distance call recently. When she finished giving the details the operator said, "Thank you for using AT & T – and I just love your accent!" Erica also answered the phone the other day only to hear the caller say, "Oh, I must have the wrong number; you have an accent."

A different accent has been a help to us here. Though occasionally we have the impression people are listening not to what we say but to the way we say it. Our words are sometimes accorded a respect they don't always receive at home in England. I think in some way we are beneficiaries of the high regard in which many Americans hold the BBC.

I must tell you that in Britain the BBC is not without its critics, with controversy over alleged political bias and the manner of its funding. It reminds me of the story of the BBC reporter who was asked to interview a Catholic priest for a religious program. When the reporter arrived at the church the priest was busy hearing confessions. The reporter thought it might be a good idea to interview the priest at the confessional grille. So after the last penitent had departed he went up to the grille and said, "Excuse me, father, may I have a word with you? I work for the BBC." The priest responded, "Thank you for coming to see me, my son. It must have taken courage to make a confession like that."

This talk today is the 200th I have given on KBOO in the last four years or so. As some of you will know, 51 of them have recently been published in book form under the title *A Different Accent.* Some people have asked me why I gave it that title.

It is first because I speak with that foreign accent. For the English this is more than just a matter of pronunciation. It is also a matter of restraint. Two Englishmen once climbed the Matterhorn and sat back to enjoy the view. After a while, one said, "Not half bad." The other concurred but added, "You needn't rave about it like a love-struck poet."

It is also the different accent of a foreigner who was evacuated to this country in World War II, who experienced firsthand the generosity of an American family who took in two young English boys for five years, treating them as their own and refusing any payment, a foreigner who witnessed the commitment and sacrifice of thousands of Americans that helped preserve a continent's freedom. It is the different accent of a foreigner who is well aware of many weaknesses and irritations in American ways at home and abroad but who refuses to surrender the belief, held by millions more overseas than many Americans realize, that this country still represents the hope of freedom and of food for a world starved of both.

There are some simple principles that help me shape what I talk about. Very early on I learned that in visiting other people's countries one should live on a basis of appreciation and not comparison. Example: you in America drive on a different side of the road, not the wrong side of the road. An American to whom I once expressed this little piece of philosophy managed to completely misunderstand me. "Oh, yes," he said, "I know what you mean. After I had been in France and Belgium and Holland and England and got back home, I sure did appreciate the United States."

I have also learned, working in some thirty countries, that human nature is pretty much the same whatever the level of education or standard of living. This nature can be changed. So, early on, too, I decided that I would try to say and write only those things that help people become different, and not by my attitudes confirm them in any prejudices they may already have. In doing so I hope to eliminate from my own life things that make it harder for others to change.

I aim with my talks to reduce polarization, the *us* and *them* syndrome, which seems the standard fare of too many conversations, to lessen fear, which I have always found to be a bad counsellor, and to heighten hope, particularly the hope that grows as you start doing something constructive about what's wrong.

In my talks I draw freely on my encounters with fascinating people I have met around the world, many of them associated as I am with the program of Moral Re-Armament. Those who have listened regularly will have realized that Moral Re-Armament has nothing to do with the Moral Majority or with nuclear disarmament. And that I am not, as I have occasionally been introduced, Michael Henderson from moral disarmament. Moral Re-Armament is not even an organization you can join. It is, put simply, a network of people of every background who refuse to play the blame game, who feel that they should not echo but alter contemporary attitudes, and who believe that any worthwhile and lasting changes in the world must begin, not with the other fellow, the other party, the other country, but with the way we live. This, too, is a different accent.

March 13, 1986

Mt. Hood 1*

In May, 1986 seven students and two faculty members of Oregon Episcopal School died during a climb on the mountain.

I CAN NEVER look at Mount Hood in quite the same way again. In its beauty and starkness is shrouded the mystery of the forces of nature and the ways of God.

It might so easily have been our precious daughter, Juliet, who lost her life in the mountain's worst disaster. As it is, family of friends whom we had just made, children we had watched on the sports fields in our daughter's teams, children we had applauded just the week before as they performed joyfully in the school play, staff members we were beginning to appreciate, are no longer with us. And our hearts go out to every one of the bereaved.

The words of an experienced mountaineer, Bob Pierce, capture what it must have been like in those hours on the mountain: "The world around you turns into a swirling, dingy whiteness in which there is no real bottom. It is hard to know if you are going uphill or down, stepping into a hole or running up against a wall. You cannot hear your friends, cannot see what is around you. The world shrinks to the immediate. You move along unsteadily in freezing isolation, every minute seeming like an hour."

The words of the book of *Wisdom* printed in the service sheet seem to epitomize the restful spirit at the Memorial a week later: "The souls of the just are in the hand of God, and torment shall not touch them. In the eyes of the unwise they seemed to die, but they are at peace."

From the fear on the mountain to the faith at the service it has been for all a painful journey. Sadness and solace, anger and love, despair and hope, have moved through many a heart, and many a tear has been shed. But as the Oregon

Winner of the Academy of Religious Broadcasting's Annual Award of Excellence 1987

Episcopal School Headmaster, the Rev. Malcolm Manson, told the nearly two thousand who attended the service and the many more who watched the live telecast, "No storm in God's creation can rival the power of the love we have felt in these last few days."

A comparative newcomer to Oregon, I can only say: what a marvellously loving community we have. I think of the heroism of those who risked their lives in search and rescue, of the commitment and skill of doctors and nurses, of the sensitivity of the media to a grieving school and its families. "The support we have received," says Oregon Episcopal School counsellor Bonnie Stanke, "will make our transition back to purposeful and joyful living a little easier."

Different images will stay in our minds for life from these days when we hung on every newscast and every edition of the papers. For some it will be the moment the snow cave was found only minutes before the search was to be called off. For some the simple illustration in *The Oregonian* of a silhouetted Mount Hood with nine crosses on its flank and the paper's editorial celebrating the spirit which took the climbers to the mountain – "the quest in a world of comfort, companionship, ease and the bright prospect to discover, in human and spiritual terms, what we are made of as individuals." For some a poignant moment at one of the memorial services. For some the courageous letter from the father of Erik Sandvik in which he said he did not wish to assign blame, expressed his support for the educational philosophy of the school and affirmed, "Erik's death has convinced me that I need to reexamine many of the decisions I have made regarding my own life. I don't know where this will lead me, but I'm thankful that, out of such an enormous personal loss, I have been galvanized into doing so. I hope that others are affected in the same positive manner."

Whether it will be from such a reexamination of our lives or from a review of safety procedures on the mountain or from a sharing of medical advances in treating hypothermia, we will all surely be beneficiaries. At the school and outside there will be frank and painful questions asked. And as this inevitable process goes forward, as the story recedes from the headlines and TV screens, as the school gets on with its business and life goes on, the supportive hands and hearts and prayers of the wider community will be needed more than ever. Not the least for survivors Giles and Brinton as they take hold of the gift of life and all it has to offer.

On June 5 a memorial rock will be placed at Oregon Episcopal School to honor Tasha Amy, Father Tom Goman, Rich Haeder, Marion Horwell, Alison Litzenberger, Susan McClave, Pat McGinness, Erin O'Leary and Erik Sandvik. It will bear the words of Helen Keller, "What we have once enjoyed, we can never lose. All that we love deeply becomes part of us."

Thanking the community for its support, as all of us connected with the school do, Father Manson said, "Please don't stop. We will need you and need you deeply in the months ahead. We have found a great treasure. In great tragedy we have come upon the soul of our school and its name is love."

May 29, 1986

Mt. Hood 2

LAST WEEK I watched the Oregon Episcopal School (OES) girls' soccer team win their first game on the opening day of the new term. Our daughter was playing. It was much more than a successful start to a new season. It was a demonstration of the resilience of the human body and spirit on and off the field.

Playing in the team was Brinton Clark who only fourteen weeks ago was hauled nearly frozen, with a body temperature in the low 70s, from the snow cave on Mount Hood in the tragedy which claimed the lives of nine of her friends. She even took a penalty kick.

Supporting on the sideline was Caroline Litzenberger whose daughter, Alison, would also have been playing if she had not died on the mountain. A courageous lady, Caroline was at one point remembering with other mothers the joyful occasion in a game last year when an exuberant Alison changed her OES shirt right on the field!

Not far away, in the dormitories, was Giles Thompson, whose pulse rate was 40 when he was rescued, whose legs had to be amputated, and who achieved his goal of wearing his new legs into school. "Why give up," he says, "you'd be in worse shape than you already are, because you'd already have lost the battle."

Tragedies, for all their inherent pain and often apparent senselessness, provide mankind with some of the most powerful expressions of eternal love and human greatness.

Last week on one particular day the front page of *The Oregonian* seemed to chronicle just one disaster after another. Nearly 400 people were feared dead in the Black Sea accident where a cruise ship was cut in half in calm sea in the dead of night by a freighter, nearly a hundred people were killed when two planes collided over a California town and crashed on a residential area, and the Warren expedition in China was believed lost. Fortunately, the latter news was premature and the expedition members are reported safe, even if their way out remains hazardous.

But that's five hundred families for whom life will never be the same again. Five hundred families with every reason to blame God, if they think in such terms, or fate, or the authorities, or the captains, or the pilots or someone. Five hundred families with grounds to sue if they have the energy and money and taste for such an ordeal and live in a society that deals with such matters in this unsatisfying monetary fashion.

That's five hundred families who will spend their lives either looking back, living in the land of what might have been, or discovering the freedom of forgiveness and a full and rewarding future.

My wife's brother, Rupert, was run over and killed by an army truck at the age of seven. The hurt remains to this day. He would have been 50 this year. We all have been close to tragedy. It could strike us tomorrow. Each of us has to decide what we do with it.

We have been fortunate over the years to get to know enough families who have been seared by tragedy of all kinds, who have grieved and yet been freed from the past, to know that anyone whatever the circumstances can find that freedom. Some have stayed in our home in Portland.

These include the former head of state of an East European country ousted by the Communists, who has found an answer to the bitterness he held against them; a Kenya settler whose father was buried alive by the Mau Mau, who is now working for reconciliation on the African continent; a Norwegian resistance leader who was tortured by the Gestapo and yet went to Germany after World War II to extend the hand of friendship; an Oregonian couple who had not one but two mentally retarded children, whose anguish has taken them out selflessly for over forty years into the lives of others.

All these friends could have lived in the past, and would probably have blighted the lives of many innocent people. But because they chose not to do so, their victories as well as their sorrows have enriched the lives of thousands.

I have just received a copy of a new video about a South African farmer friend who decided to take time daily to listen to the promptings of God in his heart. It describes the remarkable results this produced in wise farming and racial bridge-building. One sequence refers to that shattering day he and his wife discovered that their young son was deaf. As they listened in their early morning time of quiet for some wisdom on the subject, a thought came which transformed their whole approach: "Do not give your son the added handicap of bitter parents."

As I think of the valiant battle for life of Brinton and Giles, and the hopes and enthusiasms of their young friends so evident on the sidelines as students of the school, staff, and family cheered on the soccer team, I am reminded of the words of Dick Sandvik whose son, Erik, was another who died on Mt. Hood. He wrote only a few days after the tragedy, "Erik is gone and I am devastated. But I hold the hope that some people will be challenged to give our young people the love and encouragement they need to become like Erik and the friends who died with him."

September 11, 1986

Beneath the jellyfish

ST. VALENTINE'S DAY is just behind us. So I thought I would tell you the story of a young English couple who got to know each other in a Scottish castle. It was a castle complete with dungeon and moat, a colorful history stretching back 600 years, a fairy flag – and central heating. Yes, it was the first centrally heated castle in Scotland!

This was Dunvegan, ancestral home of the MacLeods, whose fortunes at that moment were in the hands of the first woman clan chief in Scottish history – Dame Flora MacLeod of MacLeod.

Dunvegan is on the west coast of Scotland on the Isle of Skye, and the social event of the year in that part of the world is the Skye Balls. The two English visitors, who only knew each other superficially, had been invited to be part of the Dunvegan party at the Balls. Others in the party included a marquis, a Member of Parliament, the daughter of the Lord Mayor of London, and a granddaughter of Lord Beaverbrook who is now a well-known actress whose face would be familiar to connoisseurs of Masterpiece Theatre.

It was definitely "upstairs" not "downstairs." But as the castle was invaded each day by hundreds of American tourists, many of them eager to establish their MacLeod lineage, it was also sometimes "backstairs." For the butler used to literally shove the house guests out of the public rooms so that these were then available to the visitors, whose entrance money paid the castle upkeep. Those with a keen nose would know what the MacLeods were eating that day.

The Sassenachs in the party, that is the foreigners from south of the border, were not reassured when they were greeted on arrival by the 86-year-old Dame Flora and informed in no uncertain terms that at the Balls the "MacLeod party do not make mistakes." So the first nights of the week were spent in rehearsing the intricate steps of the various Scottish dances which would be on the program.

The two nights of the Balls themselves were an unforgettable experience, particularly to those not used to live pipers. Looking down on the dance floor was a gallery from where Dame Flora observed the festivities which were to continue until the early hours of the morning. Next to her sat another tiara-crowned lady in her eighties. Each old lady was determined to stay awake the longest. At one point Dame Flora nodded off for an instant. In a flash the other lady rose, tapped Dame Flora on the shoulder and said ever so sweetly that she would now be going.

The first night at the Balls is always by tradition the men's night, where the Scottish men in all their ruffles and dress tartans dominate the scene. The second night the ladies wear their most colorful gowns. Englishmen, and this young Englishman was no exception, always stand out at these occasions, their wrong steps the more conspicuous because they wear not kilts but tails. "Penguins" the locals call them. For the fashion conscious, I can report that on the first evening the young English girl wore a subdued silver grey satin dress, on the second an apricot satin with a white lace top.

The young man was felt by some of the ladies in the party to be too serious, and so a plot was hatched by the wife of the Member of Parliament to cheer him up. She, however, fell ill, and the duty was passed on to the English lass. Whatever the reason, the young man certainly seemed to be enjoying himself. Admittedly shy, he took turns dancing with all the ladies in the party, but he seemed keen without making it too obvious to get his dance card marked more frequently by his fellow countrywoman. He was understood to be quite put out in the early dawn hours, when he was getting bolder but her energy was flagging and she turned him down.

After the dancing the Dunvegan party would return to the castle, snatch a few hours sleep, and then go out in a fishing boat for mackerel, which they caught in abundance. By the end of the time the Englishman was such a free spirit that at one point he hooked a jellyfish out of the water with his oar, and dangled it over his favorite dance partner. It was proof to her, she said later, that she had succeeded in her mission.

She may have got more than she bargained for, however. Because a year and a half later they were married and, like the princess in the fairy tale, lived happily ever after. Dame Flora, who died when she was 98, was the first person to hear of the engagement and always claimed credit for it. I know the story well, for the couple are Michael and Erica who live in Oregon.

February 19, 1987

Dad

I'M TOLD that in the 'thirties he used to sing a popular song, "I'm terribly, terribly British and that's what I like about me." Certainly my father was never taken for an American. I have a photo of him complete with rolled umbrella, bowler hat, gloves, and the London *Times*. In my very young days he even wore spats and, of course, if we visited him at the office, my brother, Gerald, and I had to wear hats. He was strikingly handsome.

Dad was typical of his generation, a generation that was largely lost in the mud of Mons and other World War I battles. He was there, kilted, a private in the London Scottish, although some of the family were pacifist. His battalion, I believe, were all six foot and volunteers. I still have his little rice-paper Bible that he carried in the trenches, and a letter written by him half a mile behind the front line dated March 21, 1915. He refers to the serious risks but goes on, "I would not have missed doing my bit out here for anything, as after the war is over those that return will have a wonderful experience to look back on." He adds, "I don't envy the feelings of those of my age who still hold back." He was mentioned in dispatches, and at the end of the war was a captain in the Hampshire Regiment stationed in Ireland.

Again in World War II he signed up immediately and served another six years, this time ending up as an Assistant Quartermaster General, working on the Normandy invasion preparations like the Mulberry Harbors and PLUTO, as the pipeline under the Channel was called. He, like my mother, who was an Assistant Deputy Censor, signed the Official Secrets Act and they never did, and never would, tell each other what they were not supposed to know.

I remember learning how to polish his buttons without getting dirt on the uniform, and the ritual of daily shoe cleaning. And just after the war as children we used to enjoy visiting him in the War Office and walking through the Horse Guards Arch, so that we would be saluted by those on duty. A disappointment from his war service was that he was not decorated. In the second World War he was told that he had been, but the order never came through; in the first he was offered a decoration but voluntarily surrendered it to a professional soldier in his unit.

He believed an Englishman's word was his bond and that British made was best, which was probably truer then than today. On one occasion he insisted that we all stand when the national anthem was played after the Queen delivered her Christmas message, which was normal – except that we happened at that point to be staying with a German family in a German home!

Apparently my father was expelled from his first school because he was rough with the girls. Perhaps that's why he was called "slosher" at his next one. There he had an injury that left one finger permanently stiff so he was never able to excel at cricket, though he was a fine swimmer and later represented Middlesex at rugby. He had to leave school at 15 to go into the family import-export business, starting as an office boy, making tea and filling inkpots, and eventually becoming Chairman as well as a Council Member of the London Chamber of Commerce. He would far rather, though, have been a cartoonist. All we have from that desire are sketches he did of his headmaster and of the priest who married him.

He was married twice. His first wife became mentally ill when their child was stillborn and she turned against him. He waited ten years hoping she would change. Then they were divorced. His second marriage was a very happy partnership, lasting 30 years until he died aged 68.

That was 27 years ago. We had been apart during five years of the war and much of the next four years, when I was at boarding school, and again years afterwards as I worked abroad. The older I get the more I regret the separations, and the more I wish I had had the chance to ask questions about family, about the wars, about life. How much I would take my father for granted: the way he would travel an hour to watch me play in some school game, or would bring back stamps for my collection from his many business trips to the West Indies, South Africa, Australia, trips which in those days were taken by ship and lasted weeks and sometimes months. How often I failed to say in as many words what he meant to me. I remember that when he had a heart attack and I was in West Africa my response was so inadequate that he commented to my mother, "Michael seems to think I have had a cold."

We did have rich times together. Meeting the ideas of Moral Re-Armament as a family brought us closer together. Neither for me nor for my father was it easy to be absolutely honest with each other. But we were, so there were no secrets between us. This new commitment to think for other people and for continents changed many things. He instituted a pension plan in his business which had not existed before. He developed new relations with men in the trade unions who sensed in him a new type of employer. A week before he died he was speaking at a public meeting in the East End of London about the need for change in management, and for incorruptible leadership on both sides of industry which could bring a new dimension into negotiations. He became close to leaders in newly independent nations. When he died one paper had a headline, "Friend of all races dies," and a Kenyan freedom fighter said at his memorial, "He showed me that it is more revolutionary to change a man than to cut his throat."

As Father's Day approaches I'm grateful for many things my father left us with, not the least a sense of integrity and a sense of humor. He always had a fund of funny stories. Often I find myself thinking of him when I am getting into line for some function. "Let's sit in the front seats," he would say, "before all the selfish people take them."

June 19, 1987

2 Courage personified

English writer Malcolm Muggeridge once interviewed Elsa Maxwell. "Have you met any unimportant people?" he asked. The society hostess responded, "Not until tonight."

I have met a lot of what the world might regard as unimportant people and not a few important ones as well. Some of the unimportant have been most impressive, some of the important disappointing.

Let me introduce you to people whom I have met who exemplify the words of James Keller, founder of the Christophers: "In human affairs, practically everything that has been accomplished for good or evil throughout the world began with one individual."

Lock up the silver!

AUSTRALIAN longshoremen, or wharfies as they are called, have a delightful sense of humor. It is reflected in their nicknames – "the judge" because he sat on a case all day, "bungalow" because he had nothing upstairs, "London fog" because he never lifted.

My friend Jim Beggs is no exception. I remember him speaking to students at Oxford University. "I went through Oxford, too," he said in a broad accent that almost needed an interpreter, "on a bicycle."

I first met Jim in Calcutta, India nearly thirty years ago. He was then a young trade unionist on the Melbourne waterfront. I remember playing together on a field hockey team with him. That visit to Calcutta made him realize how, as he put it, the other half lives.

Today Jim is the National President of the Australian Waterside Workers' Federation. The young man who joked that before he became active in his union the largest crowd he had ever spoken to was in a phone box, and who preferred golf and duck-shooting to union meetings, has come a long way. So has his industry. Today a handful of men on a container ship can do in 30 hours the work of 100 men working two weeks on a general cargo ship. When he started work there were 28,000 wharfies in Australia. Today there are 5,500. Jim Beggs comes to mind at this time because in the last days two publications which crossed my desk have referred to him. The first was the *Christian Science Monitor*. Last month the paper described how two million Australians tune in regularly to a radio program called "The Search for Meaning in Life." Host Caroline Jones, according to the paper, for an hour ever-so-gently coaxes Australian guests from all walks of life – politicians, musicians, unionists, businesspeople – to reveal their search for spiritual values. Her program is the Australian Broadcasting Corporation's highest-rated nighttime national radio program. It is rebroadcast three times a week, and in 1987 won the United Nations

Day Prize for radio programming dealing with peace or conflict resolution.

I suddenly noticed as I read on that she had done an interview with Jim Beggs. She asked him, "Making a decision to listen to the still, small voice, to try to discern the plan that God had for you, in practical terms, how did you do that, and how is that a part of your daily life?" Beggs replied, "We do try, my wife and I each morning, to take that time to listen and be quiet. To read something of spiritual value. . . . We began to write down these thoughts, and a new reconciliation happened between my wife and me."

The second publication which referred to Beggs was the latest issue of the international magazine *For A Change* which carries a profile of the union president. Interestingly, the profile concludes with another quote from that same radio interview. "Many people today feel rather powerless," Caroline Jones said to him. "Your way of life suggests that as an individual I do have some power to make a difference."

"I'm absolutely convinced of that, "replied Beggs. "I am an ordinary person, no education, used to be part of the apathetic majority of the trade union movement. But history is made up of individuals who have turned the tide and most of them have been ordinary people. I say to people who ask, God has a plan for your life. You may not be meant to be a leader of your profession. But if you try that experiment my wife and I made 32 years ago, you will have that peace of heart which is more important than wealth and power. You will never know the effect you have."

The profile in *For A Change* by Australian journalist Christopher Mayor describes the change that came in Beggs' life and the kind of lead he is giving in his country. When he began, he says, there was no retirement pension and "when people heard you were a wharfie they wanted to lock up the silver." Today the industry had become "the most progressive in Australia."

It was Beggs' next door neighbor who introduced him to the idea that if you wanted to see things different the best place to start was with yourself. This neighbor, who was in dock management, was a living demonstration that people could be different. The neighbor challenged Beggs to let God work through him to create a new spirit in the port of Melbourne.

Over the years, first with restitution for things he had stolen, and giving up anti-Catholic prejudice, Beggs cleared the decks for an approach that enlisted people of different backgrounds; and eventually after many attempts it projected him into a different kind of union leadership. He and his wife developed two principles: not to take sides, and to treat the union executive as a family. He believes in doing what is right, he says, no matter who gets thumped.

His leadership is not restricted to industry. The profile describes how he starts each week at seven am Monday morning meeting with a core-group of friends from different walks of life concerned about the nation and the world, and united in their desire to find out what God wants them to do.

Beggs, like other wharfies, has also been given a nickname. It refers to the first thing he put right after his neighbor's challenge. It was to return to the company a clock he had stolen from some cargo. His nickname: "Daylight saving" because he put the clock back!

February 11, 1988

A yen to serve

LAST WEEK I spoke of the Japanese statesman who gave the cherry trees to Washington, Yukio Ozaki, father of Japanese parliamentary democracy. Today I want to tell you about his remarkable daughter, Yukika Sohma.

In the 1930s Yukika Sohma was ahead of her times as, dressed in riding pants, she gunned her motorcycle through the Japanese streets. This was an era when, as she says, Japanese women were meant "to look like dolls." In recent times she has been ahead of her nation in calling attention to its responsibility to less fortunate neighbors.

A past president of the Federation of Asian Women's Associations, Yukika believes strongly that the real interests of Japan may best be served by being unselfish. "Together our countries need to live relevantly to the age we live in," she says. "What was once a proper aim for a nation is now inadequate. We cannot keep on going the way we are. Just as we need to think for other families and not just our own, so we have to care for other nations."

Which is exactly what she is doing.

After World War II when much of Japan, along with so much in the world, lay in ruins, she decided to do what she could to help bring healing, starting by accepting responsibility for the wrongs of her nation. In that period a large part of her work was in building new relations with Korea, the Philippines, and other lands which suffered at the hands of Japanese. In recent years she has also been focussing on the material needs of people uprooted by war. She says that she has never forgotten a challenge given her in the 1950s by Frank Buchman, the initiator of Moral Re-Armament, "Don't forget the needs of your Asian neighbors."

When she heard of the plight of the boat people after the fall of Saigon in 1975 and became aware that Japan had taken in practically nobody, whereas European nations who had little to do with Asia were looking after Southeast Asian refugees for humanitarian reasons, she decided to go into action. "In Japan," she says, "we had become so selfish that we were not thinking of the suffering of these people." She got together 20 or 30 senior Japanese as a board for an Association to Aid Indo-Chinese Refugees. The press heard of her efforts. She told them that she wanted to help the refugees *and* the Japanese, that if Japan kept closing her heart she would become isolated from the rest of the world, that Japan needed to trade to survive and for trade needed friendship, and that one way to do this was to open the purses not just of the rich but of the ordinary people. On the spur of the moment she had the thought to ask every Japanese to give one yen. She said this on television.

The response was amazing. One man offered her his office. Friends came and worked voluntarily. And within three months she had reached her target of 110 million yen, one for every Japanese. The *Japan Times* headlined her words, "I found a goldmine in the hearts of the Japanese people." "There are many individuals who want to care," she says, "and I have been learning to tap the resources that are hidden in each." After her success in raising money for the boat people, Yukika felt she needed to keep open the hearts which had been opened. "Otherwise people sleep on what they have done," she said, "and then they forget."

She discovered that the Cambodian refugees needed housing because their huts had been burnt. She found that bamboo houses could be built for 20,000 yen each (less than $100). So she launched a second appeal with the theme: "Don't you want a second house – in Cambodia? You won't be living there but we'll put your name on it." Again the public responded. She heard that it had been cold last year in Southeast Asia, so with the help of the major newspapers and NHK Television she asked for one thousand tons of clothing for a million refugees in Thailand and elsewhere. She gave a time limit of two weeks and enlisted two transport companies with 80,000 agents all over the country. The company presidents put up posters announcing that any package addressed to the refugees would be transported at half price. The target was exceeded. She also received more than 30 million yen for the shipping costs, and she went personally to Cambodia last year to deliver the first thousand tons.

"I am often tempted to feel that I can do things myself," she says. "I have accepted that I cannot do anything worth-while in my own strength. All I need to do is to be prepared for God to use me. Japan, too, tends to think she can do things on her own but needs to learn to serve the world. I am committed to see this happen. The challenge is to accept God's commission and let go of ourselves."

Yukika Sohma was recently decorated by the Emperor

for her services to the nation over the years. Last year she was also the recipient of an award from the Korean President for her long years of fostering friendship between the two nations.

But she is not resting. She is now extending her work to helping refugees in other areas, including Afghanistan. Her constant theme is that there is a battle to fight between right and wrong in our hearts, a choice we have to make daily. "We all come from developing nations in the spiritual and moral sense and we can learn together,' she says.

As adviser to the Japanese Prime Minister on the status of women, she is setting a fast pace herself.

April 18, 1985

Sullivan's principles

PRECIOUS NICKEL in hand, the ten-year-old black child entered the drugstore in Charleston, West Virginia. He went up to the counter, sat on a stool, and ordered a hamburger. "Black boy, stand on your feet," said the white man behind the counter. "You can't sit down here." It was Leon Sullivan's first encounter with bigotry and discrimination. "I decided," he said later, "I would stand on my feet against this kind of thing as long as I lived." And he has.

As we enter Black History Month we might spend a moment on the life of this 6'5" Philadelphia pastor who has indeed affected history.

From an early age he was involved in the Civil Rights movement. At 21 he was elected President of the National March on Washington Movement, forerunner of the Freedom March of 1963. After the Supreme Court ruled that segregation was illegal he was at the heart of the Selective

Patronage Movement that in four years turned around the hiring practices in Philadelphia without a penny spent on litigation, a public meeting held, or a poster carried.

This experience heightened his already growing conviction that blacks urgently needed training as well as opportunities for employment. With the purchase of an old jailhouse for one dollar a year for 99 years, he launched the Opportunities Industrialization Centers that subsequently spread to 140 communities and have trained more than half a million school dropouts in job skills.

In 1971 Sullivan joined the Board of General Motors where he supported the first shareholder resolution calling for the company to withdraw from South Africa. After a visit to South Africa he began to draw up a code of conduct for U.S. businesses operating there. Now known as the Sullivan Principles, they call for desegregation in the workplace, the improvement of training and promotion prospects for blacks, and the upgrading of health, housing and education facilities. In the course of eight years, companies pledged to the adoption of these principles spent around $230 million on black education, housing, legal aid, and other social causes.

But last year, dissatisfied with what he felt was the failure of even his strengthened Principles to shift the South African government into genuine racial power-sharing, he announced that he was calling on U.S. firms to leave the country. When I interviewed him the day after this decision, he told me that his priorities were changing, that he might no longer be so preoccupied with South Africa.

His greatest satisfaction, he said, came from having provided thousands in the United States with training and jobs, and he now wanted to expand that overseas where he had already established training institutions in a dozen African countries and an International Foundation for Education and Self-Help.

Earlier this month Sullivan announced that he would be retiring from his Baptist pulpit to get behind these concerns. When I spoke to him last week, he told me, "I'm going to the next phase of my life – a more global ministry and effort to help train and feed the poor of Africa and the developing countries."

If Sullivan's track record is anything to go by, he will make a difference there too.

February 5, 1988

Buried alive

THIS HAS BEEN a vintage year for anniversaries. We won't see its like again until 1995.

The ending of World War II, in Europe first and then after the dropping of the atomic bomb in Asia, and the founding of the United Nations, were events of supreme importance. And all sorts of people, particularly those concerned about the contemporary arms race and the Holocaust, have used the 40th anniversary to make points for today.

Many sincere people feel that keeping a great wrong alive in the minds of succeeding generations may help prevent the recurrence of anything similar. They may be right. Though in many places around the world it is the keeping alive of the remembrance and bitterness of the past which is fueling division and preventing settlements.

I have a feeling that the hand of friendship and the power of forgiveness, not because we have forgotten but because we have remembered the full horror, is a potent remedy we have not fully explored.

I was struck last week by the frank statement of the Japanese Prime Minister at the United Nations charter anniversary meeting. Yasuhiro Nakasone, a wartime naval officer, apologized to the 159-member body for Japan's role in World War II. "Since the end of that war," he said, "Japan

has profoundly regretted the ultranationalism and militarism
it unleashed, and the untold suffering the war inflicted upon
peoples around the world and, indeed, upon its own people."

As AP correspondent, O. C. Doelling, wrote, "Nakasone's apology was unusual in a hall where many other
commemorative speakers have used the occasion to attack
their country's foes and to defend their own policies."

A few weeks ago some of us watched a film *Voice of the
Hurricane*. It was about a white settler family's attitudes and
emotions just before Kenya's independence. Last week that
Kenyan experience was brought dramatically home to us by
one of the Leakey family.

Speaking at Portland Community College, Agnes
Hofmeyr, who now lives in South Africa, said that when the
fortunes of Mau Mau were on the wane a "prophetess"
declared that the gods were angry and had to be placated by
the sacrifice of a good white man.

Agnes' father, Gray Leakey, a friend of the Kikuyu people
who spoke their language and never carried a gun, was
chosen. Sixty Mau Mau broke into the family farmhouse,
killed her stepmother and also their cook, because he was
Christian, and carried her father up Mount Kenya where he
was buried alive as a human sacrifice.

When Agnes heard the news she became very bitter,
feeling she never wanted to have anything more to do with a
black person, and tempted to throw overboard her Christian
faith. But as she reflected in quiet she had the clear thought,
"I should have no bitterness or hatred, but work harder than
ever to bring a change of heart to black and white alike, no
matter what it costs."

A short time later she had a chance to apologize to a
meeting of thousands of Kikuyu for the selfish way white
people like her had lived and to tell them of her decision.
Many responded by saying that they would take up that
struggle with her. "What was left of my bitterness melted,"
she said.

More recently a former Mau Mau leader, a senior man
in Kenya, admitted to Agnes that he had helped plot her
father's murder. He had been one of the group who selected

him for killing and, he added, had since been one of another group who had selected a Leakey cousin of Agnes to be a candidate for Parliament. This cousin was now the one white man in the Kenya Parliament and a junior minister. "A circle of healing had happened," she said.

"Thank goodness for the power of forgiveness that we can work together," says Agnes. Out of a tragedy had come one of the most precious experiences in her life, which enabled her to give what was needed now in South Africa. "Tragedy can be used to bring healing to a nation."

Memories, and anniversaries, can rub raw wounds, or as in the case of this Kenya settler and the Japanese Prime Minister, help build a different future.

October 31, 1985

Unarmed among headhunters

I FIRST MET Alice Wedega 35 years ago when she was representing her country at a conference in Ceylon, now Sri Lanka. Nearly twenty years later we were her guests in her beautiful country, Papua New Guinea. Alice was the first woman member of the Legislative Council and the first woman in her country to be decorated by the Queen of England.

At a dinner welcoming the Queen to Papua New Guinea, one of the Queen's bodyguards heard that Alice had visited Northern Ireland and asked her why. In her direct fashion, she told him that in the early days her great grandfather was a cannibal. "At that time," she told him, "our people used to kill and eat men. They would practice payback. That is, if one of your side killed one of mine, my side would kill one of yours. But the missionaries came from Europe to stop us doing all that. And now I have been back to Northern Ireland to help the Europeans there stop doing it."

I have just heard that Alice has died, and thinking of this story I realized afresh what a colossal leap into the modern world the Papua New Guinean people have taken in an incredibly short time, and also that perhaps a more primitive people may have something to teach us in the West. The answer for payback, or retaliation, or tit for tat is surely one of the most needed elements today whether it is in Palestine or Sri Lanka, or in street gangs or even on the soccer field.

When I was a teenager I was impressed by a story told me by a missionary about how headhunting was stopped in an area of Papua. It was only years later that I learned that Alice was one of the courageous people who contributed to that story. It was also the story of Western missionaries who were so different in their approach than many that they were not even regarded by some local people as white.

It began in the mission station of Kwato founded by Charles Abel in 1891. He was a farseer and different from most missionaries of his time, feeling the need to develop the practical as well as the spiritual life of the villagers. Even in those days he looked forward to the time when Papua would be a self-governing nation. Today grandchildren of the first Papuans educated by him are in public service in Papua New Guinea, one of them heading a diplomatic mission.

When Alice was young she was trained at this mission. Then she was sent to Australia as a servant, the only way Papuans at that time could go overseas. This was a disastrous experience, and she hated the Australian woman she worked for.

However, in the 1930s a new dimension came to the Kwato mission, as those there learned to listen for God's guidance and measure their lives by absolute moral standards of honesty, purity, unselfishness and love. Seeking direction from God Alice found an answer to the resentment against the white Australian woman and as a result against all whites.

At this time it was decided that those at Kwato would go out to the other villages around and share their experiences of how the good spirit had changed their lives. Before long rainmakers had changed and destroyed the things they used to make magic, sorcerers went to the homes of people they had killed and asked for forgiveness, women were no longer the property of men, children were wanted and cared for, people lost their fear of each other, and polygamy was naturally ended. People built new houses, cleaned their villages, and got together for "power house," as they called it, times of listening and prayer that became part of the life of whole villages.

Then, courageously, the Kwato people moved out to the remote villages of the headhunters who were causing problems for the government. Alice and her friends went unarmed. "We did not try and teach these people," says Alice. "We let them find from the good spirit what he wanted them to know that day. In fact *dawalia*, finding, was the word that was used for listening to the Spirit's directions. It was amazing to see how fast the experience spread. Sometimes a whole tribal group would ask forgiveness for the things they had done wrong." After one peace *fest* 84 men who had been headhunters sent a message to Kwato about their change. The Lieutenant Governor commented that since Alice and her friends had been there he had not had to try a single case.

Alice wrote down the amazing convictions of these headhunters acquired through listening to the good spirit, and then during World War II buried them for safety. Luckily they have been preserved and are incorporated in her autobiography, *Listen My Country* (Pacific Publications). Its foreword is by a former Papua New Guinea Governor General, Sir John Guise, who had known her since 1928. He could vouch for the stories of change because his own wife's aunt was one of those murdered before the men changed. Guise calls Alice's life "a challenge to the leaders and youth and men and women of this nation."

It is interesting to consider that these headhunters, who learned to discern the direction of the good spirit, had no education, could not read and write, and had never heard of the Ten Commandments. Do we sometimes complicate things in our Western society, and fail to recognize when the good spirit is speaking to us? Or do we recognize but fail to obey?

Alice concludes her book, "Papua New Guinea will never be a country without problems, but it could be known for the way we get over them."

January 7, 1988

A corpse looked back

IF YOU HAVE not lived through the "kingdom of night," as he calls it, you can probably not fully comprehend the motor nerve of a man like Elie Wiesel. If you have not seen your close family members taken away to the gas chambers and furnaces, and witnessed absolute evil firsthand, as this Rumanian-born Jewish novelist did, you may have difficulty accepting the single-minded passion of a survivor dedicated to keep that memory fresh for the world. But you cannot escape his moral eloquence.

An emaciated face looks out at you from a 1945 photograph. Can he be only 16? No wonder Wiesel ends his first book *Night* (Avon) with this reaction as he first saw himself in a mirror, after he was freed by American troops from the Buchenwald concentration camp: "From the depths of the mirror a corpse gazed back at me. The look in his eyes, as they stared into mine, has never left me."

Some 42 years and 24 books later, that "corpse" was in Oregon to speak at Linfield College. A world celebrity, honored, listened to, the writer, now an American professor and a recipient of the Congressional Gold Medal of Achievement, a husband and father, is still on a crusade against what he believes is the world's greatest sickness, indifference —

indifference to God or to man, to life, to suffering, or to happiness and unhappiness. There is an urgency to his writing and to his speaking. As he says in one book, pointing out that survival was often determined by being a minute too early or a minute too late at some place, "Those who survived know they must do something with every minute of their lives."

The face in the mirror, deeply lined and in repose somewhat sad, came vibrantly alive as Wiesel spoke to a two thousand capacity crowd, his words studded with anecdotes and with a surprising amount of humor. The occasion was the Third Annual Oregon Nobel Laureate Symposium. The theme was "Building a moral society: the Holocaust and beyond."

Wiesel is, indeed, a survivor, not only of Ausschwitz and Buchenwald but also of the temptation later to commit suicide. And he has twice held tickets for planes that crashed. He is a man of faith in God and his creation despite his searing experiences. But, as he told one questioner last night who sensed a change in him over the years, "I may have a different tone but the content is the same. The questions which plagued me are still open. Not a single one I can answer. I don't understand humanity, inhumanity, God's law. It's still an open wound."

Accepting the Nobel Peace Prize in 1986 Wiesel said, "I swore never to be silent whenever and wherever human beings endure suffering and humiliation. We must always take sides. Neutrality helps the oppressor, never the victim. Silence encourages the tormentor, never the tormented. When human lives are endangered, when human dignity is in jeopardy, national borders and sensitivities become irrelevant."

Again last night he attacked "the complicity of the bystander." His indignation is not restricted to the sufferings of World War II and of his Jewish people. Though he feels it important to remind people of the uniqueness of the Holocaust, drawing the important distinction that even if all victims in the World War II camps were not Jews, all Jews were victims, his concerns have ranged from the suppression of Solidarity in Poland to the plight of the boat people from Indo-China. At the Symposium he referred to his unsuccessful initiative to get Gorbachev and Reagan to address the nuclear dangers by meeting in Hiroshima.

Elie Wiesel looks back on a life of questions not answers. He is not apologetic for that, as he believes that only totalitarian states claim to have all the answers. "In a moral society," he said, "the questions and answers are always in *your* hands." He cannot hate but he will not forgive. This master of words explained to me that, poetically speaking, silence rather than words would have been a more eloquent condemnation of Nazi atrocities, for the use of words can sometimes devalue the horror of the Holocaust. But he has felt morally compelled to speak up.

Certainly few have used words to greater effect in a cause than he. He claims to speak only for himself. But he is surely a worthy spokesman for the "mutilated dreams and visions" of the millions who perished. "One person of integrity can make a difference," he believes. And he has, and still does, to judge from the ovation he received last night. Elie Wiesel is, as he was introduced, "a messenger to all humanity."

April 28, 1988

What a great God

A BRAVE RUMANIAN pastor recently spoke in our home. He is the Rev. Joseph Tson, President of the Rumanian Missionary Society, living in Wheaton, Illinois, from where he broadcasts and distributes Christian literature and relief and medical aid to his country. There had come a time four years ago, after he had documented cases of illegal government interference in church affairs, when it was no longer safe for him to remain in Rumania.

In 1977 he was imprisoned, charged with treason, and beaten. Returning to his cell, he recalled it was Holy Week and was suddenly filled with the privilege of sharing Christ's suffering. When he was taken for interrogation the next day, he said to his jailer, "I am sorry for shouting when you beat me. I should have thanked you for the most beautiful gift – to suffer as our Lord did. I am praying for you and your family." The beating was stopped and he and his five friends who were imprisoned with him spent that Good Friday morning together, holding a service. "It was the most beautiful Holy Week in our lives," said Tson. He told his captors, "Your strongest weapon is killing. My strongest weapon is dying. Only, when you kill me I am the victor."

In 1955 Tson was given what he described as "a very special book, a rare book that influenced my life like no other." It was *For Sinners Only*, about the Oxford Group and Moral Re-Armament. That book, he said, was more than the story of Frank Buchman and his conversion, more than the story of a group. "It was a training in quiet times in the morning and in capturing the thinking of the Lord." He had learned from it that he should get up much earlier in the morning. "I got up at 5 and have stayed with that all my life," he said. "I get up for a study of the scripture and to listen to what God has to say to me, how to tackle that problem, or that difficult person. I get in a frame of mind where the Lord can speak to me."

How could one be sure that it was guidance and not just wishful thinking, he asked. He suggested four tests: is this pure, is this honest, is this out of love, is this unselfish? If it passed those tests, it was of the Lord. This practice of Bible study and waiting for the Lord had then become one of the most important aspects of his life.

Fourteen years later he applied for permission to visit a friend in Vienna and was interviewed by a secret serviceman. During the interview he had the clear thought that he was meant to go to England and study in a first class seminary. He and his wife and others talked it over and felt the idea was of God. "Here's what happens when you follow guidance," he said. His visa permitted him to visit Austria. He got a friend in England to invite him for two weeks to Oxford. Now, the British were not allowed to give him a visa unless the Rumanians had already stamped permission in the passport. Tson went to the British consulate in Vienna where they completely failed to notice that permission was missing and granted the visa. When he got to England the Foreign Office people were amazed. "It's incredible," an official told him. In Oxford Tson was immediately offered a scholarship at Regents Park College. "Guidance was to study in a first class seminary," he reminded us. "It was one instance of God's guidance. You have to have a training of your ear so you can capture the voice of the Holy Spirit."

He emphasized again the importance of checking thoughts against those four tests. For instance, he said, a man who had been indebted to him turned against him and threatened to publish his sins to the world. As Tson shaped what to reply, the Lord said to him, "If you write this letter that way it won't be from the Holy Spirit." So he asked in quiet, "How should that letter be, if dictated by the Holy Spirit?" It became clear that he should write, "Thank you. I will double the list of my sins, listing sins not known by others and across the list I will write, 'The blood of Jesus Christ cleanses us from all sin.'" The man wrote back apologizing instead of getting into a fight. "Listening to the Holy Spirit is one of the most beautiful things in my life," said the pastor. "All we have done in Rumania was following that."

He described some of the things they had done. When he got back from Oxford in 1973 he felt he should write a paper about the state of church freedom in the country and what should be done about it. He showed it to an engineer friend, Aurel Popescu, now Pastor of the Rumanian church in Gresham (Oregon). Popescu said, "It is beautiful. It is marvellous. It is impossible. They will kill you." Tson knew that he was called to be a watchman for the Church. He had to blow the trumpet. He had to do what God said. "The only word was obedience."

Tson gave a copy to the Secretary of the Baptist Union

who showed it to the secret police. Tson was fired from Baptist Seminary, harassed, forbidden to preach. Part of his paper was published by Keston College in England, the foremost research institute on religion in Communist lands. For three months, he said, he was in no-man's-land.

This was the moment, however, in 1973 when Rumanian President Ceausescu came to the United States to beg for most favored nation status in trade relations. Acceptance was conditional on human rights. So the US government handed Ceausescu Tson's document as a test, asking if he would solve the problems as outlined in it, reducing government interference in the church. The President accepted the conditions on a Friday. By Tuesday Tson had his job back and the churches a greater degree of freedom. "I got that guidance in May," said Tson. "I believed I was committing suicide but I wanted to obey God. How could I imagine that God could take that paper via England to the President within six months and give unbelievable victory. What a great God we have. He takes your little obedience and does these miracles. And it all started with training in the Holy Spirit's guidance."

September 26, 1985

3 In a lighter vein

I live in the state of Oregon which prides itself on being environmentally alert and a pioneer of recycling.

I regard my commentaries in the same light, a contribution to a better total environment and a vehicle for recycling all the sensible things said and done by others. I would tend to agree with Blaise Pascal who wrote three hundred years ago, "All the good maxims already exist in the world, we just fail to apply them."

A cartoon in *Punch* depicted a minister preaching. The caption was his reassuring words to his parishioners: "If your life style is going to be seriously affected, then of course disregard everything I've said."

No such disclaimer comes with this book.

An English revolution

YOU AND I, are very lucky people. Though let us not become linguistically lazy because of it. We speak the world's principal language, English, along with more than a billion other people, nearly a quarter of the human race. English is the official language of sea and air, the language of popular culture, international commerce, and world diplomacy. Why, there are even some English people who believe it's the language used by God! In China, whose Mandarin language comes second in the list of most widely used languages, more people are learning and speaking English today than in the whole of the United States. English and Mandarin are followed, a long way behind, by Spanish, Hindi, Arabic, Bengali, Russian and then 2,796 other languages.

Of course, we don't all speak the same English. Varieties of pronunciation, of spelling and of usage abound. Opinions vary as to where the main stream flows and where the purest strain is to be found. But according to no less an authority than Robert Burchfield, the editor of the *Oxford English Dictionary* whose final supplement has just been published, American English is "the most important branch of English today."

As you go around the world you note the varieties of English, and you can tell whether someone learned the language from radio braodcasts and, if so, whether they were tuning in, for example, to the American Forces Network or British Forces Radio, or whether they learned English from conversation with foreigners or from reading period novels or textbooks. I remember how surprised I was when I was once thanked by a Bombay Indian with the words, "I say, you are a brick," – words which no doubt came straight out of an English schoolboy tale of a generation earlier.

You are struck in your travels, too, by interesting colloquial expressions. When I used to phone a government office in Nigeria and the person I wanted was away from his desk, the person who answered would invariably say, "Not on seat, sir," – a most graphic way of putting it. You also

note valiant efforts to cope with the language which aren't
entirely successful. A Norwegian was introducing a learned
professor at an international conference and wanted the audience to know that this man had a very broad outlook. "This
is Professor Skard. His thinking is all over the place."

This fall Public Television will be airing a nine part series
on "The Story of English," tracing its development from its
origins with an obscure European tribe to its present global
predominance. Filmed on location in sixteen countries on
five continents, the series will be hosted by Robert MacNeil
who spoke enthusiastically about it on a recent visit to Portland. The different segments will look at everything, he said,
from the influence of Scots emigrants who arrived in Appala-
chia via Northern Ireland to the current contributions being
made to the language by black English.

"The Story of English," as its publicity material says, "is
the story of a world journey, of a language literally
conquering air and space, land and seas, to make this an
English-speaking world." The heroes of the story are not
only famous writers like Chaucer and Shakespeare, Dickens
and Twain, but also the ordinary people who have,
throughout the ages, added to the richness of the language
and carried it with them throughout the world. "In the last
1500 years, and against all odds, English, a crafty hybrid,
survived invasion, neglect, and suppression to become the
first truly global language in the history of our planet."

Philip Howard, the Literary Editor of *The Times* of
London has written an entertaining book entitled *The State
of the Language – English Observed* (OUP). A classical
scholar, Howard is the author of many books and widely
known for his occasional columns about the English
language "New words for old." Fortunately, for me at least,
just when his erudition is making me think I should revert
to a simpler book, he employs some delightfully earthy turn
of phrase, retails some revealing anecdote, discloses some
fascinating historical insight and I just have to read on. It
takes perseverance, a dictionary and a sense of humor – but
for anyone who loves the language it is worth the effort.

"There is an English revolution going on," says Howard,

"but it is healthy, manageable and on the whole beneficial." English is going through more rapid changes than ever before as the world accumulates more knowledge, more words, more slang. When the first three volume edition of the *Encyclopedia Britannica* was issued, he says, there were plenty of people around who knew everything in it and some who knew a great deal more. Now, just talking of dictionaries alone, it was no longer possible for a polymath, or a Renaissance man, or a crossword puzzler, or even Dr. Johnson himself to carry in his head a working knowledge of most of the English lexicon that mattered.

In his book the worthy wordsmith deals with everything from dialects to clichés, from GodSpeak to PopSpeak, from Franglais to Strine, and even with the use of "hopefully." He writes of the gobbledygook jargon of sociologists where an informal chat becomes "a relatively unstructured conversational interaction" and of *Time* magazine journalese: "Backward ran sentences until reeled the mind." Slang, he sees as a "sign of healthy growth." English, he says, is stuffed as full of foreign words and phrases that have become clichés "as a London Underground train in January is stuffed with flu germs."

But, just as you are enjoying the fact that a twentieth of French is made up of anglicisms and that *Le Monde* uses one English word in every 166, he comes in with the devastating judgment, "As far as one can judge, from rhymes and other clues, the American accent and stress of English is more 'correct', i.e. older, than the British accent. Shakespeare and Queen Elizabeth I spoke English that sounded more like a modern American than a modern Englishman."

If this sort of thinking catches on, I may have to give up radio commentaries.

August 14, 1986

Encounters of a royal kind

IT WOULD BE HARD to imagine a more incongruous scene. We were sitting last year in a back corner of a restaurant in a small Arizona town. It was called "The Horny Toad." At the bar lounged a few characters who looked as if they had stepped out of a Marlboro ad. No one took any notice of us – an older couple, a nun, and my wife and me – as we munched on our cheeseburgers. I wonder what the other customers would have thought if they had known that our fellow diners were a king, a queen, and an archduchess. We rather enjoyed, as I am sure they did the anonymity.

No such luck, however, for the visitors to Washington, DC this week who I heard described on TV as the best known couple in the world.

When England's King George VI and Queen Elizabeth visited Canada many years ago they were given a civic reception in a certain Canadian town. King George was fond of recounting a conversation the Queen had on that occasion. She leaned over to the mayoress and remarked that in England mayors always wore chains at such functions. Didn't they have them in Canada? "Yes," replied the slightly flustered mayoress, "We wear them too." And after an embarrassed pause added, "But just for special occasions."

No one in Washington, DC seems under any illusions about the current royal visit not being a special occasion. Nor does anyone seem neutral.

I must admit the fascination of Americans with our royal family while pleasing me mystifies at the same time. I noted that syndicated columnist Jeff Greenfield described the passionate desire of some Washingtonians to hobnob with Prince Charles and Princess Diana in these words: "And now men and women who can move millions of dollars at the snap of a finger, entrepreneurs who summon tens of thousands of jobs into existence with hard work, new ideas, and tax credits, are reduced to a pack of pathetic beggars, all for the chance to come within shouting distance of a young couple who might, but for the accident of birth, find themselves lining up for food stamps at a local council hall in Liverpool."

He says that the root of what he calls a mania is the constitutional provision prohibiting the granting of titles of nobility to Americans. And he suggests that America might get into the business of selling titles. "If we are really so bedazzled by the spectable of nobility," he writes, "let's bring some of it home and raise a few billion dollars for the Federal treasury while we're at it." As for him, he says, he'll stick with the royalty he's already learned to admire – Count Basie, king crabs, and Duke Snider.

Columnist Melvin Maddocks writes, "Let's be frank. We Colonials have an attitude problem. Like all revolutions, our revolution led us simultaneously to overrate and underrate what we overthrew. One knee involuntarily genuflects. One side of the mouth involuntarily sneers. We are in a royal state of democratic confusion." Another columnist, Charles Krauthammer, sees little reason to save the Waleses, as he calls them. He concludes an article, "Dinner with Di? If you like cotton candy. I prefer steak. Give me brunch with Clare Booth Luce."

Prince Charles and Princess Diana and other members of the royal family do encounter a lot of criticism, much of it scurrilous. By tradition they cannot answer back. When *People* magazine did their malicious "Malice in the Palace" article this summer, I wrote to the Palace for some information. The reply from the Queen's Assistant Press Secretary stated, "I am afraid that articles of this nature do appear from time to time and we feel that they are best ignored."

Though regarded by some as overpaid the royal family, through encouraging tourism, probably bring more money into Britain than anyone else. The present trip will boost buying British. The Queen and the Duke of Edinburgh are greatly respected in Britain, particularly for the example they have set for family life. And Prince Charles is increasingly speaking out, despite constitutional restrictions, on important issues, most recently for instance on poverty and homelessness.

I've never met the royal couple and probably never will.

But I did have one close encounter with the family. Two other bachelors and I who were contemplating getting engaged decided to go for a walk and a talk in Richmond Park. We were strolling in the Isabella Plantations when I suddenly saw corgis coming towards us and, in the distance, Princess Margaret admiring some roses. We quickly left that part of the gardens thinking we were trespassing and took refuge on a bench in the woods. Well, as you may have guessed we soon saw the royal corgis coming towards us again, followed by Princess Margaret and Queen Elizabeth, the Queen Mother. What do you do? What's protocol? There was no Miss Manners to ask. We jumped up and, because we did so, the royal party came over to talk to us. I can't report a profound conversation. But I will tell you that three bachelors returned home convinced that this was a good omen, and within the year we were all married.

November 14, 1985

Old age is unexpected

MY UNCLE Bill is a man of life-long convictions. He is a Christian and a pacifist. In the First World War he worked with refugees instead of serving in the military, in World War II he was involved with radium in medical research. This was supposed to be at the risk of shortening his life. I don't know whether it has or not, but he has just celebrated his 91st birthday.

Since 1919 Bill, a chemist, has been involved in running Christian boys' camps in England, devoting almost all his vacations to the task. Over the years boys have attended from 200 schools, and I remember an archbishop in West Africa telling me the important influence they had in his life.

Though severely handicapped by arthritis, Bill continues to take part in the aspects of the camps where physical prowess is not required, and he remains the accompanist for services and sing-songs. That's 68 years of uninterrupted, unremunerated service to young people.

In a society where even youngsters are encouraged to be thinking of retirement benefits, I am heartened by the spirit of 90-year-olds I know who have little time to be preoccupied with how they're doing; they lead such full lives, even when restricted by physical limitations of all kinds.

Trotsky, the old Soviet revolutionary, once said, "Old age is the most unexpected of all the things that happen to a man." I guess he was speaking from theory as he was only six years older than I am when he was murdered. But I know what he means. A retired Canadian editor, Brian Tobin, recently described some of the observable phenomena in *The Torch*, an alumni newsletter in Victoria BC. "At first kids get up to give you a seat," he wrote. "Shop girls use that gentler tone of voice reserved for the white-haired. But when mature adult ladies offer you their bus seats you know things are getting serious. You're old! . . . Almost unnoticed at first, little changes are taking place. The laws of the universe are being altered for you. For one thing, you enter upon a new battle against gravity. Things are always dropping when you barely touch them. Anything left near an edge will fall over it. Most things that you carry will slip from your hand. Pencils, pens, paper clips and buttered muffins are hit by an extra bolt of gravity and head for the earth's center no matter how careful you are. And they're hard to find. They can hide right in front of your eyes.

"I met a friend the other day," he wrote, "I don't know how old he is – about 75 I guess – middle-aged. He told me about losing a shoe one morning, just as he was about to put it on. He was pretty vexed about losing it – said it belonged to a set!'

Tobin ended his piece, "A little five-year-old from across the street comes over to talk to me now and then. One day I had to keep saying, 'Pardon? What was that?' She said, 'Your ears don't listen very well, do they.' I explained that when people grew old they often couldn't hear what was said. Her answer: 'Well, you look old, but not *that* old.' I guess," says Tobin, "I'll settle for that."

This newsletter was sent me by Mary Hamilton from Victoria, BC. She writes me at least once a month, takes an interest in world affairs, and her latest letters and a phone call were all about how to get my radio commentaries into her local paper. She has a lively sense of humor. Earlier this year she had a serious operation for which the average hospital stay is from ten to twelve days. She was home in ten and the next day sat at her table for breakfast, lunch and dinner — which is not bad considering she is not as young as her clear handwriting would suggest. She is 95. Before she went in for the operation she said, "No flowers, no visitors, I'm just going in on business. . . . It's much ado about nothing. They'll fix me up and I'll be as good as new . . . I'm in the hands of the Lord and what He wants to happen will happen. After 95 years I can't complain. I think he has done a pretty good job of looking after me."

She is very much in the tradition of John Wesley, of whom it was said on his 86th birthday by Robert Southey that his strength was "now dimmed so much that he found it difficult to preach more than twice a day."

Another Hamilton, Julia Hamilton, no relation, a great lady in Seattle I visited recently, will be 90 in the new year. She lives in a retirement home on Lake Washington. In younger years she roamed the world. Her husband was an American ambassador. Now her eyesight and hearing are failing but not her spirit and her interest in people and the world. Indeed, when I recently had dinner with her and she was drawing me out on many matters, I realized that with my combination of an English accent and a raised voice to be sure she heard I was soon having an audience that went way beyond our table. She continues to follow everything that's going on and even, a few weeks ago, wrote President Reagan with a practical suggestion how he could improve relations with Libyan leader Gaddafi.

Her mind now roams the world from her retirement home

and she has written a poem which begins with these apt and expressive lines:

My life could be filled with trivial things,
Clouded in sound and sight.
But I am so glad my mind still has wings,
And my heart and my spirit are free to take flight.

Some time I must tell you about some of the younger kids on the block, the spring chickens, the 80-year-olds.

One other note on age: An older friend of mine who felt his memory was going decided to go to a healing service to see if it would help. The only trouble was that when he got to the church, he says he couldn't remember what he had come for.

December 4, 1986

Polls apart

THERE WAS an uncharacteristic moment of silence on a TV talk show the other day. A guest was stopping to think. The host quickly stepped in to gloss over the glaring gap. "I am glad you are taking a while to answer," he said.

It was "Firing Line" and William F. Buckley, Jr. had as his panel three top English journalists. The interview was filmed in the offices of London's *Sunday Telegraph*. Buckley's first question, directed to the paper's editor-in-chief, Peregrine Worsthorne, was, "How is it that, if the reports from a recent poll are correct, as many as one third of the British people believe that the nuclear peace is threatened primarily by the United States?"

After his pause, which must have seemed more like minutes than seconds to the producer, Worsthorne said that it was a difficult question to answer because he didn't feel that sophisticated television interviewers should base questions on poll returns which were almost always meaningless. He had taken his time to come to terms with "a third of the people think" because he didn't believe a word of it. In fact, he thought that 99% of the British people would share with the United States the view that it was a good idea to contain the Soviet Union, indeed that relatively few people in Britain would question the view that the Soviet Union was an evil empire.

Whether all would agree with Worsthorne's assessment or not, what interested me even more than his disputation of anti-Americanism was his distrust of polls. I must admit I share a skepticism about the accuracy of even honestly conducted polls. Almost every time I am confronted by a survey or polled through the mail or on the telephone I am dissatisfied by the alternatives. Pollsters are always trying to crowd me into a box where I don't comfortably fit. Yet the results of such questionnaires are confidently projected or extrapolated or whatever it is they do, to turn the views of a few hundred randomly selected individuals into the firm convictions of hundreds of millions of concerned Americans.

I mentioned my reservations to a pollster in a local shopping mall last week. She assured me that my views would be accounted for under "indecisive." It wasn't quite what I had in mind! She quickly went on the attack, extolling the virtues of polls. "Unless you give your opinions nothing's going to be changed," she told me. She handed me a brochure from her company – one of six hundred such research companies in a Galluping growth industry. "Since relatively few people are selected for each survey," it says, "the opinions of those who participate are looked at with great interest by those who can make a difference in the products and services that we all use."

I suppose I am fortunate that being a foreigner and not a registered voter and often recording an insignificant earning power I am the target of fewer canvasses than many, or at least find it easier to deflect the challenge to my privacy. I don't have to employ the dodge suggested by columnist Jonathan Nicholas in *The Oregonian* recently. There's a phone call. "Good evening," says the voice, "we're taking a telephone poll to . . ." You interrupt: "Oh, really. I hope you don't have to carry it far."

I concede that even allowing a generous percentage for sampling error, I am poles apart from most Americans in my reaction to our poll-arized society. The Roper Organization, who, of course, would hardly be biased, found through a poll that 75% believe most opinion polls work "for the best interests of the general public."

There was a lighthearted but penetrating treatment of polls in a recent episode of that brilliant English TV comedy "Yes, Prime Minister." Because of a poll the Prime Minister wanted to introduce national service. His advisers wanted the opposite. The way to change his mind? Commission another poll. The first poll went something like: "Are you concerned about the rise of crime among teenagers, do you think there is a lack of discipline in schools, do you think young people welcome structure and leadership, do they respond to a challenge, might you be in favor of reintroducing national service?"

The new poll would go something like, "Are you worried about the danger of war, are you unhappy about the growth of armaments, do you think there's a danger in giving young people guns and teaching them how to kill, do you think it wrong to force people to take up arms against their will, would you oppose the reintroduction of national service?" The prime minister's secretary on whom both series of questions was tried responded "yes" each time. "You see, Bernard," his civil service boss said to him, "you're the perfect balanced sample."

I appreciated a cartoon in the *Sydney Bulletin.* "We're doing a post-election survey," says the questioner. "Which opinion poll did you vote for?" I am surprised at the fuss over election exit polls* here. Whatever happened to the secret ballot?

---

* *Asking people on the East Coast, how they voted means that, with the three hours time difference, national results can be predicted before the polls in the West even close.*

Wouldn't it be a new day if every voter treated every pollster like, well, a polecat. The problem would vanish. Just supposing all of us refused to be sampled; we axed the polls, so to speak, and there were no ratings. Politicians could say what they really believed. TV producers could go for quality programming. There'd be no new products we didn't need on the market. I guess I'll have to run that idea up the pole and see who salutes it.

Yes, I do share the perspective of the English editor, as I do of the policeman who once arrested the man who got us into this mess. It was in 1948. George Gallup had just predicted a win for Dewey in the presidential election and was stopped for driving the wrong way up a one-way street. The cop read the name on the driving license. "Wrong again," he said.

January 15, 1987

Trickle-down theory

IF YOU EVER want an example of the weakness of free enterprise, I recommend to you a study of the great American faucet. At least it seems a weakness in so far as the consumer is concerned and proves that the trickle-down theory of economics has its limitations.

I had thought that I had plumbed the depths, knew all the twists and turns of taps, until my recent experience at the Minneapolis airport.

There's an animal in Dr. Doolittle's menagerie called a push-me pull-you. It's what I often want to call American faucets. Because you never know which you have to do to get water out of them. I wonder how many other visitors to these shores have shared the experience of my wife who on more than one occasion has just given up and gone washless.

There's the kind you pull out and the kind you push in, there's the kind you turn to the left and the kind you turn to the right. There's the kind you tilt down and the kind you tilt up. Remember to tilt before twisting. There are levers you maneuver to left or right. There are some that separate hot and cold and others that mix them and ones, usually in the shower when you have soap in the eyes, that you turn the wrong way and are scalded.

And, of course, they come in all designer shapes and color-coordinated hues and are even advertized on television to appropriate sounds – like Handel's Water Music.

In public restrooms I have come across those that are activated when your foot touches a button under the basin. And then there's the cutting edge of Minneapolis!

Confronting the faucet in all its elegant, its streamlined functional simplicity, I could not figure out what I was supposed to do. There were none of the telltale clues I have come through experience to recognize. As luck would have it, I put my hands under the spout, and a jet of water spurted forth. I removed my hands and it stopped. How the heck could I have guessed that! (Actually, subsequent research at Portland airport makes me think that it is distance from the wall rather than closeness to the faucet that primes the pump, so to speak.)

Was I just a stupid foreigner who didn't understand American ways? I stepped back to watch the great unwashed as they came in. No, they had the same trouble. After observing a few handwringing would-be handwashers, their fruitless efforts, and their puzzled mien, I stepped forward to tell successive men, who sounded pretty American to me, how to cope with the latest tap technology. They were both relieved and grateful.

Come to think of it if you could station a man or woman at each public faucet to tell people what to do, you could solve any unemployment problem overnight.

Of course it won't be long before faucets are voice-activated and you will be able as you enter a bathroom to predetermine the temperature of the water you want. I wonder how they will handle translation.

Methinks that in this land of the free I do protest too much. The freedom of the faucet is after all a precious one. We don't want any Communist regimentation, all of us condemned to use one serviceable, predictable grey monotone dispenser of what, to my great dislike, one local TV weatherman has come to call its heavenly counterpart "little drippy drops of H_2O."

March 25, 1988

What farmers know

I think that I shall never see
A billboard lovely as a tree.
Indeed, unless the billboards fall,
I'll never see a tree at all.

UNFORTUNATELY for Ogden Nash he didn't live in Oregon, a state which, I have heard, is still the best place in the world to grow trees. It was good to note last Christmas how increasingly Oregonian tree farmers are supplying the world with Christmas trees. I wonder if they realize that they should make Queen Victoria's husband, Prince Albert, their patron saint. For he probably more than anyone else popularized the Christmas tree in England, from where the idea spread rapidly.

I talk about trees today because we have just started Oregon's annual Arbor Week. I stress week because most states as far as I know are satisfied with an Arbor Day.

I don't know much about trees. I'm a big city boy. In fact, when I first moved here nearly eight years ago, I noticed some Portlanders looked a little taken aback when I would say, "It's nice to move to a small town like Portland." I have been more interested in the Douglas branch of my family tree – it's my middle name – than in the Douglas fir on which the economy of Oregon largely depends.

However, a tree farmer friend of mine asked me to speak to his service club, and after I had agreed, he said, "You can talk about anything you like, provided you talk about trees." Since then I have taken a close look at a lot of processed trees, books that is, and absorbed quite a bit of tree lore.

In a book about Prince Charles and Princess Diana I read Charles' words after he had planted a tree in Sydney, Australia: "Whenever I plant a tree, it's next to one that either my mother or father planted ten or twenty years ago. I've noticed the trees my mother plants tend to flourish, while the trees my father plants tend to wilt and die. And I can't think of any explanation for that, apart from the fact that trees must be snobs." In that context it is interesting to record that the writer Pope said 200 years ago that "a tree is a nobler object than a prince in his coronation robes."

It is just as well that it was a woman writer who described a tree as "an object that will stand in one place for years and then jump in front of a lady driver." I rather like the line from Stephen Vincent Benet, "The trees in the street are old trees, used to living with people, family trees that remember your grandfather's name."

We had a poet from Australia staying with us, Michael Thwaites. His poem "Forestry" goes:

My love and I in all agree
    As one, save this thing only:
While she likes trees in silver clumps,
    I like them huge and lonely.

In this our hearts divided stand
    As Egypt and the Pole,
Though in all else we are not two
    But one consenting soul.

And that is why we love to walk
When Night, the blackbird, perches,
Together, counting I the oaks,
And she the white young birches.

To be serious for a moment there may be something those
who care for trees, and those who live in farming communities, may have to say to our present society and its values.
Two thousand years ago Cicero quoted the words, "He
plants trees to benefit another generation." And 250 years
ago Thomas Fuller wrote, "He that plants trees loves others
beside himself." St. Bernard said, "You'll find something
more in woods than in books. Trees and stones will teach
you that which you can never learn from masters."

What are these people talking about? Oregon tree farmers
will know better than I. But I'll venture a few thoughts. We
live in a shortcut society. We want results without commitment. We want profits without care for people or land. We
want instant this and instant that, with microwave meals
and scrape-of-the-ticket lottery winnings, instant solutions
for world problems, instant wisdom in thirty second TV
bites, along with our instant tea and coffee.

Perhaps our greatest failing is our preoccupation with the
present, in a material and a religious sense. Too few have
any wider perspective; to use a most inappropriate metaphor,
we don't see the wood for the trees. Perhaps our greatest
need is to learn what the farmers know, that you have to
take the long view, that often you are sowing for the enjoy-
ment and profit of others, that you have to cooperate with
nature and with God, not work against them, that you have
to be patient.

I had a farmer friend in Kenya, Jack Hopcraft. When he
started farming he accepted a very simple philosophy. Within
five years, living and farming on the basis of that philosophy,
he transformed a derelict farm into a model used by the
Agricultural Department as a demonstration for right
farming practices. Among other things he put in a system of
broad-based contour terracing to forestall erosion, built a
village of good quality brick dwellings for his workers and

their families, and planted more than 20,000 trees on the place. That was forty years ago.

His philosophy? "Farm this piece of land as if you will be farming it forever but live your life as if you will die tomorrow."

April 2, 1987

Travel travail

MODERN TRAVEL has been cynically described as "breakfast in London, lunch in Istanbul, supper in Delhi – and your luggage in Rio de Janeiro."

I am often bemused at the way Americans prepare for travel abroad. It is an object lesson in serious intent. (It has taken me a little while to adjust to the fact that you can get college credit for looking at English ruins.)

Obviously travel abroad needs looking into carefully these days. It isn't necessarily the moment to go to the Baalbek Festival in Lebanon. Though when Americans started cancelling their trips to Europe because of fear of terrorism, I inwardly enjoyed the English newspaper comments that pointed out that Americans were statistically likely to live longer in Europe away from American roads.

Every country seems to be getting in the business now of helping its nationals behave better or sell more effectively in foreign countries. The German government last year, for instance, with German thoroughness issued a 128-page booklet of holiday trips and urged the burgers to show tolerance, patience, and friendship to all.

The Japanese External Trade Organization is even tougher on the reader. It published a 276-page volume to make life easier for foreign businessmen in Japan. For instance, how to bow to a Japanese when trying to make a good first impression: "The bow is property executed from the waist, with the arms at one's sides and thumbs parallel to the seam of one's trousers. The back should remain straight. Do not change the angle of your head." The book also passes on the advice, "If you take out a Japanese company chairman for a round of golf, it is better manners to lose."

The British government gives out two prize-winning booklets. They are called *Get it Right Before You Go* and *Help for Exporters*. The prizes were won in a competition for Plain English. *Get It Right* lists eight things consuls can do and eight they can't for the 20 million Brits who go abroad each year for pleasure or profit. It warns against carrying parcels through customs for other people and says, "Hobbies, like bird watching and train, plane and ship spotting can be misunderstood, particularly near military installations."

The American government is no slouch in these matters. The State Department for all of 100 cents will give you its publication *A Safe Trip Abroad*. Its advice ranges from "If possible, book a room between the second and seventh floor – above ground level to prevent easy entrance from outside, and low enough for fire equipment to reach" to "If you're in a situation where someone starts shooting, drop to the floor or get down as low as possible; don't move until you're sure the danger has passed."

In the book's foreword there is, however, this reassuring word, "Foreign travel can be a rich and rewarding experience and the odds are very much in your favor for an incident-free trip."

So, to first timers planning a summer vacation abroad I say, "Come on in, the water's warm." But I must add a caution, as one who has sat through more slide shows of returnees from foreign shores than he wanted to. Bear in mind the comment of American journalist Elizabeth Drew who said, "Too often, travel, instead of broadening the mind, merely lengthens the conversation."

March 11, 1988

4 Peacemaking

The rush and pressure of modern life are a form, perhaps the most common form, of its innate violence. To allow oneself to be carried away by a multitude of conflicting concerns, to surrender to too many demands, to commit oneself to too many projects, to want to help everyone in everything, is to succumb to violence. More than that, it is cooperation in violence. The frenzy of the activist neutralizes his work for peace. It destroys his own inner capacity for peace. It destroys the fruitfulness of his work, because it kills the root of inner wisdom which makes work fruitful.

Thomas Merton

There is a true majesty in the concept of an unseen power which can neither be measured nor weighed. There is harmony and inner peace to be found in following a moral compass that points in the same direction, regardless of fashion or trend.

Ted Koppel

Peace at a fair price

WHENEVER I hear of culture, a certain person once said, I reach for my gun. I have the same reaction sometimes about peace. Well, not exactly. I'm as much a peace lover as the next guy, many of my friends are in the peace movement, and sincere and dedicated they are. But I do react as more and more new groups jostle for attention, and I wonder whether a concentration on peace, admirable as it sounds as an aim, cannot sometimes lead us astray.

I suspect that if the peace movement had been more successful in Lincoln's time he would not have been reelected and we might today have two ununited States of America; and if the peace movement had been less successful in Europe in the 1930s Hitler might have been deterred from going to war. And what about the perspective of a German Member of Parliament who stayed with me in Portland? "Do you know who the real peacemakers are?" he asked. "It's the 300,000 US troops in Europe. Everyone talks about peace; they keep it."

There are some 250 peace organizations in Oregon. We have peace marchers and peace knits and now a peace train. We have nuclear free villages and shadow paintings on our sidewalks, peace churches and peace studies and peace institutes, and everything from PAND to WAND not to mention Gophers for Peace and Justice. And some who may have thought it was all getting a bit too earnest have launched hedonists for peace, or is it hedonists for social responsiblity? I can't remember.

Frankly I rather share the perspective of columnist Georgie Anne Geyer who is more afraid of being killed by axes or handguns than of nuclear war. And I would go along with Archbishop William Temple who used to describe how he·was lying awake in bed one night, weighed down by the burdens of the world, and it was as if the good Lord touched him on the shoulder and said, "William, you go to sleep. I'll keep awake." It is sad to see peaceworkers having burnout. It shouldn't be that way. They surely should be the first to be at peace, and, as William Sloane Coffin reminded us last week, to keep a sense of cheerfulness.

I believe the most effective peacemakers are not those who shout the loudest or frighten you the most or demonstrate the most dramatically, but those who live in a way that spreads peace and who work to answer the hatreds and the legacies of history which are the seeds of new wars. This is, indeed, the vineyard in which many long-established peace groups have labored for years, and done so in a way that transcends themselves and their politics. Peace is, after all, a fruit of people becoming different, of new attitudes within and between nations, and has comparatively little to do with weaponry. It is in part, as Saint Augustine pointed out, the right dynamic ordering of public life, and in part a patient concern not to upset the precarious balance of international relations and a nation's security. It begins with the person we don't get along with and is not furthered by setting people against each other or in a spirit of blame. Peacemaking needs everybody.

November 20, 1987

Patron saint of hostages

TERRY WAITE stands out in a crowd. And I don't just mean his 6′ 8″, 220-pound frame. A local friend of mine, Andrew Hay, who met him some years ago before he had become a celebrity tells me that it was clear even then that here was an outstanding individual.

Since January 11 (1987) there has been no confirmed news of his whereabouts, and concern grows for the safety of the Archbishop of Canterbury's secretary, whom the Catholic Archbishop of Liverpool calls one of "the prophets of this age of violence." To return on a fifth visit to Lebanon after the revelations of White House arms deals would be to court danger for any Westerner, but especially for one so associated with attempts to free hostages.

Waite, however, is ready to risk his own life if he thinks that the safety of others can be procured. He treats courage with the nonchalance that characterizes his encounters with individuals. Another friend who has met him says that despite his size he is not intimidating; his handshake, like his voice, is gentle, his direct gaze conveys interest and kindness. Waite describes himself in terrorist situations as apprehensive but not much frightened and certainly not paralyzed. One English paper editorialized on his captivity, "It is unlikely that personal danger will weigh much in his lone but not lonely thoughts."

The 47-year-old Anglican layman is used to risk. As adviser to the first African Archbishop in Uganda he was held at gunpoint during the crisis following the expulsion of Asians by President Idi Amin. In Iran he was conducting a service for British detainees when armed revolutionary guards stormed in. In a memo to his secretary several years ago he stated that if ever he were missing no one should come after him: "There must be no ransom paid if I am kidnapped." The British government, which through its ambassador in Beirut made it clear it did not wish this unconventional diplomat to return to Lebanon, has made it equally clear that there will be no deals for hostages – even Waite.

Among his interests Waite, who dislikes desk work, lists walking and travel in remote parts of the world. For two years he was coordinator on the Southern Sudan Relief Project, and he has been an international consultant on missionary and development work for the Roman Catholic Church. He is fond of music, particularly Mozart, is acutely interested in international affairs, and is a member of the Lefthanded Society. In recent years, before trying to free hostages, he travelled with the Archbishop of Canterbury on overseas tours and pastoral visits. He and his wife, Frances, have four children.

Waite has been associated with the release of ten hostages in the Middle East, four in Iran, four in Libya, and two in Lebanon. They include two Americans, Lawrence Martin Jenco and Benjamin Weir. When he obtained the release of the Britons in Libya in 1985, the English daily, *The Guardian*, wrote, "All diplomatic missions rely to some extent on the personal qualities of the envoy, but Mr. Waite depended entirely on them."

He offers no money or guns and has little worldly authority behind him, yet, as David Winder writes in the *Christian Science Monitor*, "His credibility as a successful Middle East negotiator is widely recognized as second to none."

This stems from his ability to keep confidences and to establish contacts on a personal basis, from an infectious humor which comes to the rescue in tricky diplomatic situations, and from a sensitivity to national sensitivities. It is shortsighted, he believes, to react to terrorism and not ask what makes these people do what they do. His perspective comes in large measure from his belief in the importance of a religious approach to life. Of his dealings with the Libyan leader, for instance, he says, "With Colonel Gaddafi I was trying to establish three very simple attributes of God to which we could both subscribe – God as a God of compassion, mercy and justice."

A book, *Lent for Busy People* (Bible Reading Fellowship), includes Waite's meditations on the prophet Isaiah. He says that Isaiah is pointing to a relationship of harmony and compassion that is often lacking in our mechanical understanding of international affairs, where we seem totally to fail to apply the principles which we say are moral. "If we were to practice the same morality in our interpersonal relationships as we practice in international relationships," he writes, "we wouldn't dare to step outside our own front door. So what about having a clearer and deeper examination of the whole area of international morality, and nations being big and generous enough to feed the flock of others? So that nation really does 'speak unto nation.' "

Some newspapers, while encouraging prayer for the envoy's safe return, have said that he should never have gone and should never go again. The English *Catholic Herald* believes it's not worth endangering his life among fanatics "who are immune to the sweet reasoning the Primate's emissary is good at dispensing." The London *Sunday Telegraph* even writes, "Lambeth Palace (the Archbishop's office) must realize its saintly meddling in Middle East intrigue is no less dangerous than Machiavellian freebooting from the White House basement."

The waiting and prayerful public and the Waite family can, however, be proud of "this contemporary folk hero of the British people," as one American paper dubbed him. He has been decorated by the Queen of England, granted audience by the Pope, and nominated by a group of British Members of Parliament of all parties for the Nobel Peace Prize for 1987. A colleague at Lambeth says that Waite makes him think of one of those great Victorian explorers who went striding across Africa: "In a curious way, that's one of the reasons for his success; he does things other people would think impossible." *People* magazine called him the "patron saint of hostages."

There is, obviously, a limit to how much personal diplomacy can be undertaken on a basis of personal trust. But we can be grateful that there are some, like Terry Waite, who are willing to dare to extend that limit.

April 30, 1987

Out of the present darkness

FORTY YEARS ago Japan was facing starvation. Rice had virtually run out. Her people, however, were prepared to face death rather than give in. This willingness to fight was such that reasonable estimates by the Allies put the cost of invading Japan at a million Japanese dead and 200,000 Allied soldiers killed.

Then the Allies dropped the atom bomb. The news was suppressed in Japan, and the cabinet sat in session for two days deliberating what to do. Some were for continuing the struggle but finally they decided to surrender. The question then was how to communicate the decision to the Allies, and how to tell their own home-based troops without touching off a revolt. Only the Emperor, it was clear, would carry sufficient authority. But he had never broadcast, his voice was not known. Would people feel it was a hoax?

A cabinet meeting was convened in the Palace. The Emperor agreed to broadcast, and preparations were set in train to record him in the Palace. But the news leaked out. Some officers tried to get troops into the Palace to overpower the Emperor's guard. They shot the commanding general and began a hunt for the tape which had by then been completed. Failing to find it they went to the radio station but were again foiled as volunteers they had called for arrived too late. At seven they listened to the Emperor's broadcast on the radio as he asked the nation "to accept the unthinkable, tolerate the intolerable and bear the unbearable." The officers went outside and committed *harakiri*. "Japan's longest night was over," as one account put it, "and the Emperor's voice heeded."

Interestingly, I was with a man in Washington DC recently who says that within hours of the surrender, when the desperate food situation in Japan became known, he was called by President Truman and asked to organize immediate food shipments. Within days ships began leaving West Coast ports with the one commodity which was nourishing, available in large quantities, and easily transportable – peas. They were already in warehouses, frozen, ready for the winter markets. Older Japanese remember the time when they lived on peas and little else. It tided them over. A friend of mine, Katsuji Nakajima, who was in Hiroshima when the bomb exploded, was one of a group of 70 Japanese who visited the United States in 1950. He was then a leader of the Metal Workers Trade Union and had hated the Americans as he had hated the bosses. But he had found an answer in his life to blame. "The removal of my hatred," he said, "was to me an even greater spiritual shock than the physical shock I received at Hiroshima."

Just five years after the atomic explosions, nine years after Pearl Harbor, this Japanese group was received in Washington DC. Their spokesmen addressed the House and Senate, the first Japanese ever to do so. In the Senate Chujiro Kuriyama, representing the Prime Minister, thanked the American people for their aid. "We are sincerely sorry for Japan's big mistake," he said. "We broke almost a century-old friendship between the two countries. We ask your forgiveness and help." The Senators gave him a standing ovation. An Australian member of Parliament who was in the gallery said that after the Japanese apology in the House there was "a hush, the most intense silence I had ever encountered, because everybody appreciated this was something which, very shortly before, no man or woman living would have thought possible."

The *Saturday Evening Post* commented, "The idea of a nation admitting that it could be a mistaken has a refreshing impact. Perhaps even Americans could think up a few past occasions of which it could safely be said, 'We certainly fouled things up that time.' " The *New York Times* wrote, "The mayors of Hiroshima and Nagasaki were among today's visitors. If they, too, felt they had something to forgive they had achieved that miracle (of enemies becoming friends). For a moment we could see out of the present darkness into the years when all men may become brothers."

The Mayor of Hiroshima, Shinzo Hamai, was interviewed at that time by CBS Radio. "We people of Hiroshima," he said, "hold no bitterness towards anyone, because we have realized that this tragedy is naturally to be expected from war. The only thing we ask of the world is that everybody becomes aware of what happened in Hiroshima, how and why it happened, and exerts every effort to see it will not have to happen again in any other place."

When Mayor Hamai returned to Hiroshima he refused, despite considerable pressure, to put on the monument to the bomb an inscription of blame. Instead he chose the words which are there to this day and which I saw 25 years ago, "Sleep in peace; we shall not make the same mistake again."

August 8, 1985

A quiet night in Beirut

A SCANT HALF MILE from the devastated "green line", the road to Damascus which separates the Muslim and Christian communities in Beirut and where from time to time we see on TV young men shooting at each other from amidst the rubble is where my friend Fuad lives. I call him Fuad for the sake of this talk; to reveal his real name would be dangerous.

The French-style *immeuble* in which he lives is pock-marked by shrapnel and overlooks the embattled Museum area. High explosive shells have exploded above and below his fifth floor apartment. An American who stayed with him before the exodus of foreigners says that during his first night there he was awoken several times by machine gun fire alternating with the occasional thump of a mortar. Fuad greeted him at breakfast, "I hope you had a good rest. I'm grateful it was a quiet night." Fuad had insisted at great personal risk on meeting him at the airport which meant going through five check points on the way home.

Fuad is a serious, slender lawyer, with black almost crewcutlike hair. In appearance owlish, in his ways precise, he was once described by a visitor from France with the comment, "Now there's a brain." Rooted in the village and yet with the intellectual training of a graduate of the Jesuit University of St. Joseph's, Fuad is typical of many of his Maronite Christian community.

He is trying to help Lebanon by reaching out to other communities. His determination is fueled by the belief that if someone does not do it, his country will go to ruin. Mistrust characterizes the city's life. Muslim mistrust of the Maronites goes back to the years when Fuad's community collaborated with the Crusaders, to their linkage with foreign Christians, and to the fact that in times of crisis they have turned to the French for material and spiritual support.

Some years back as token of a new approach Fuad had the idea, which he believed came from God, to seek out the Mufti, the leader of the Muslim Sunni community, to apologize for the way his people had conspired to keep the reins of power in their hands, not permitting the Muslims to be fully responsible for the country.

Fuad apologized to the Mufti for his people's attitude and said he wanted to accept the changes in his own life which would help create a new Lebanon. The Mufti rose and shook his hand: "What you say is the one ray of light in the present darkness. Thank you."

The next day, Thursday, the Al Aksa Mosque in Jerusalem was set on fire and feelings ran high. Security forces were doubled in the streets of Beirut for the Friday prayers in the Grand Mosque. But nothing happened, for the Mufti's sermon that day, according to the Falangist paper *Kata'ib*, was a "model appeal for brotherhood and understanding."

After the devastation of the Israeli invasion Fuad saw the Mufti again. He said he was sorry for the killings in the camps and renewed his pledge to work for a new country. Again the Mufti thanked him, embraced him and assured him of his support.

Until he was stopped from doing so by the rigid division of the city, Fuad regularly visited Muslim friends. Now he meets every two weeks with his Christian friends in East

Beirut, last week with 70 of them. Once or twice a year he also meets for several days in Cyprus with people from the Shia and Sunni and Druse Muslim communities as well as with Catholic and Protestant Christians. Recently he arranged to have shown on Beirut television, in French with Arabic subtitles, the film, *For the Love of Tomorrow*, which is about reconciliation and forgiveness between French and Germans after World War II.

Fuad's courage to reach out in this way – he has even surrendered the gun he used to carry as he believes in a non-violent solution – stems from the change that came in his life when he decided to accept absolute honesty, purity, unselfishness and love as guidelines in life and the daily discipline of listening for God's guidance, principles he found in Moral Re-Armament. The change began with honesty and restitution for cheating in his university exams, the returning of library books and a new frankness with his family. As he took these simple moral steps he began to get ideas for his country.

By trying to follow the whispers of God's guidance Fuad may have saved his own life. He seeks guidance even on what route to take through the city. He certainly saved the life of the Swiss ambassador who later, in gratitude, gave a dinner for him in Switzerland when he was there to attend the Moral Re-Armament World Assembly.

So next time you see Beirut on the nightly news be heartened to know of the likes of Fuad who are quietly and courageously at work – and perhaps say a word of prayer for their safety.

March 19, 1987

After the killing fields

THIS WEEK A LIVELY Cambodian lady sets off on a confidential mission to a South Asian country where she has been invited, as a Buddhist, to be part of an effort to break down suspicions between different religious and ethnic groups.

A few years ago that would have been impossible for her as she was eaten up with bitterness towards the Khmer Rouge, the Cambodian communists.

Renee Pan was born and raised in Cambodia but had to flee to the United States when the Communists took over her country in 1975. The following four years were years of terror in Cambodia. Almost three million Cambodians were killed. Renee lost all her relatives except her three children and her husband who may be alive or dead, she does not know.

It was hard for her to forgive the Khmer Rouge for what they did to her family, friends and beloved country, but the burden of revenge she carried for a decade was lightened, she says, from the moment she did so.

As a refugee she struggled first to become economically independent, and then began to give of her time to work for the welfare of her community and country. She was encouraged to do so by remembering what her parents had told her as she grew up. Good deeds received good deeds, they would say, and, quoting Buddha, a good deed would follow you like your own shadow while bad deeds were like the trace left behind by the wheel of an oxcart.

As well as helping South-East Asian refugees settle – Renee serves on the Minnesota State Advisory Council on Refugees – she became politically involved in the Khmer People's National Liberation Front, the KPNLF, which is trying to help her country free itself from Vietnamese occupation.

But she reached a point, she says, where she did not have anything to give. "My energy did not regenerate itself," she recalls, "my brain was empty and my heart was numb and insensitive. I got angry very easily, hated bad people, was unhappy, selfish, and did things foolishly."

She realized one day that her mind was consumed by what her Buddhist religion sees as the "three fires of the world" – greed, anger and foolishness. She decided each day to have a time of quiet, to provide, as she calls it, "an indispensable food to nurture my mind." Through having quiet times, the teachings of Buddha became real for her for the first time. "It became less hard," she says, "to endure the discipline that leads to enlightenment."

Renee had become discouraged by the divisions within the KPNLF because they undermined its effectiveness. She wrote to many of the key leaders expressing her discontent and putting the blame on them. She had hoped to clear up the situation but this action only seemed to create more mistrust.

In order to bring unity Renee decided to meet the KPNLF president and apologize to him. "I was ready," she says, "to accept the consequences without fear of losing face or friends." As well as making a verbal apology, she wrote a letter which was made public. "Finally, the pardon was given," she says. "I felt such relief." And, far from losing friends as she had feared, she was admired for her action. "I am sometimes accused by other Cambodian friends of supporting the Khmer Rouge because I refuse to accuse them." she says. "But if I kill the Khmer Rouge, I will become one of them."

The experience of quiet times and change also affected her family. "In our tradition it is not easy for an adult to ask for forgiveness from a younger person," she says. "It took me quite a while to do it, especially with my own children."

Renee is now in the process of finishing a project called the Cambodian Children's Education Fund. Its goal is to enhance the work of existing organizations concerned with the education of the Cambodian children living on the Thai-Cambodian border. Up to 2000 teachers are waiting for teacher-training workshops which she hopes, if all goes well, to get started in the spring of 1988. Eventually, 40,000

children will benefit from the project. She wants one day also
to have the opportunity to use her training and experiences of
change with the Vietnamese as well.

As an economic forecaster for a pool of power companies
in the Twin Cities, Renee is a computer specialist. She likes
to use computer images to describe what has happened to
her. Human memory, she maintains, is unlimited when
compared with computer memory, but if the memory is
loaded with impurities, it is unable to solve even a simple
problem. "Forgiveness freed some megabytes in my
memory," she told a conference recently. "I dare to solve
problems on a larger scale, with less CPU* time, in a more
efficient way."

If anyone has something to contribute in bringing erstwhile enemies together, surely it is Renee Pan.

September 17, 1987

Red repentance

I HADN'T THOUGHT of it until someone pointed it out to me.
For some three years now there has been practically no word
of Red Brigades terrorism in Italy. Whereas we used to read
with painful regularity of the murder of people in Italian
public life. The assassination of former Prime Minister Aldo
Moro was a particularly shocking example.

Have the activities of the Red Brigades just been crowded
out by other terrorist activities or has the public got so used
to their crimes that newspapers are no longer reporting them?
The answer to both questions is no, and the true reason is
both highly encouraging and largely unreported. I have just

* *Central processing unit*

been reading it in an article in the English Catholic weekly, *The Tablet,* headed "Red Repentance." It is by a New Zealand Jesuit, Gregory Jordan.

In 1980, it appears, Vittorio Bachelet, a Professor of Law, and President of Catholic Action, was shot dead by a woman member of the Red Brigades. Because of his eminence Bachelet was given a State funeral which was seen by millions on television. At the service the murdered man's son, Giovanni, forgave his father's assassins personally, and at their express wish, on behalf of the whole family. The congregation, instead of responding in a traditional manner, was silent and then burst into applause.

"The repercussions of that more-than-human gesture," Jordan writes, "were felt even in the ranks of the Red Brigades, and the first to be touched was the young woman who had fired the fatal shots."

Jordan says that he first heard of this story at a students' conference, from an archbishop who told him that this act of forgiveness had so struck the terrorists that it became a turning point for them. "It even led them to inform on militants at large, thus enabling the security forces to break the power of at least that generation of the Red Brigades."

Over the last years the murdered man's brother, Father Adolpho Bachelet, has developed a growing apostolate among former terrorists. He has built up a network of contacts with some 150 to 200 former terrorists in Italian prisons. Some have completed their sentences and are being helped back into society. Former extreme Left-wing terrorists who had never been baptized have now asked for the sacrament. They have been married in the Church and had their children baptized. In one church there was even a mass of reconciliation between a victim's family and the man who had led the assassination team.

Father Bachelet, according to *The Tablet* article, insists that the Bachelet family was not the only one to make a public act of forgiveness or to evoke a response from the terrorists. But after three years work he did receive a letter from eighteen terrorists inviting him to visit their prison.

"We want you to come," they wrote, "so that we can

listen to whatever you want to say. We remember very well what your nephew said at his father's funeral. Those words of his keep taking our minds back to that ceremony where life triumphed over death, and we too were overcome. In the aftermath we were deeply touched, and kept asking questions, trying to find within ourselves what were the roots of our transformation. The reason why we tried to change was the example you – the family – gave us; it made us realize that it was possible to live another way."

January 28, 1988

Don't curse the French

THERE IS SPECULATION WHAT COURSE Tunisia will take when the rule of 83-year-old President-for-Life Habib Bourguiba ends. The country has done remarkably well in the last 30 years despite few natural resources and a population explosion. An energetic reformer, Bourguiba has transformed an impoverished state into "a model of third-world development," according to Louise Lief, writing in the *Christian Science Monitor*. But the pro-Western country faces serious problems including Islamic fundamentalism, the corruption that can accumulate in a one-party state, and radical neighbors, Algeria and Libya.

Bourguiba has ruled Tunisia since independence in 1956. And as political observers consider the future this might be the moment to reveal the remarkable story of how the country achieved that independence without the bloodshed which overtook Algeria. For, as Bourguiba himself once said, "Each time that men by negotiation and good will succeed in finding an answer to the conflict of powerful national interests, the whole world from East to West should pause for a moment in silence, meditate on the lesson and draw from it fresh inspiration."

One of Bourguiba's colleagues in the fight for independence was Mohamed Masmoudi, later cabinet minister and ambassador. He had been condemned to death by the French and was living, as he says, with "the demon of vengeance" and "as stuffed with hatred as a bomb is with explosives." Committed to violence, he was working with French Marxist organizations, questing "how to make the task of government impossible."

This was in 1953 when the nationalist Neo-Destour movement, headed by Bourguiba, then in prison, was demanding complete independence from an obdurate French government. "It was in this political climate," wrote Diane de Watteville-Berckheim in the book *Le fil conducteur* (Editions Alsatia) "that an event took place which was completely unknown to the press and whose consequences were unforeseeable."

That summer Masmoudi accepted the invitation of a French journalist whom he trusted to go the Moral Re-Armament conference in Caux, Switzerland. To his surprise he met there French men and women who were different than he was used to. He learned what had gone into creating reconciliation between France and Germany. He felt his hatred slipping away. He said publicly that in the spirit he had found there agreement could be worked out with the French. While he was in Caux his 80-year-old mother had written him a letter which ended, "God bless you, my son. God curse the French." At the end of his stay at Caux, Masmoudi replied to her, "God bless me, mother – yes. I need it. But don't curse the French. I have found French with whom we can work without distrust for justice in our problems and aspirations." He told her that he had decided not to travel to Libya or Cairo to organize the armed struggle from there, but to return to Paris.

Over the next months with his own people, as he traveled the length and breadth of Tunisia, and with French people in Paris who had heard of his change of attitude, the groundwork was laid for a meeting of minds. He met French leaders like Schuman, Pflimlin, and Mendes-France, who had become Prime Minister and was open to a new way of doing things. He met French who as he says "would previously have avoided me like the plague."

An occasion at the Moral Re-Armament center in Paris was pivotal in the subsequent developments. At the instigation of M. Chevallier, Mendes-France's Secretary of State, Masmoudi and Jean Basdevant, responsible for Tunisian Affairs at the Foreign Office, were invited for dinner. At the last moment Chevallier couldn't attend because of a cabinet meeting. It was only then that he mentioned that neither of the guests, who had never met, had been told that the other would be there. It could have been disastrous. But such an atmosphere was created and such a spirit brought to the table by Masmoudi that the two men could talk frankly and without recrimination.

Shortly afterwards official negotiations began between France and Tunisia. And Masmoudi, not yet 30, was appointed one of his country's representatives to talk with Basdevant and the French delegation. Both men were accompanied by their experts and, reports de Watteville-Berckheim, they had "to negotiate less with each other than with the members of their own delegations." The negotiations took nine months. Masmoudi says, "With the standards of honesty, purity, unselfishness and love inside oneself, even if another appeared dry, closed to all discussion, one ended up getting access to his heart." Whenever the atmsophere became too tense the discussions would be suspended, and Masmoudi and Basdevant would walk around the ministry gardens and seek together the best way out of the impasse. Another member of the French delegation said later, "We were often embarrassed by Masmoudi's integrity."

Later, after the negotiations had led to his country's independence, Masmoudi made a statement in Washington DC that but for what he had learned through Moral Re-Armament his country would still be engaged in a war without mercy with France. This was corroborated by Basdevant who said, "Publish it." And Bourguiba said, "The world must be told of the effect of Moral Re-Armament on my country."

I was present a few years ago when Masmoudi told this story in Paris. At that time he was Ambassador to France. "I was but one of the instruments in disentangling the events," he said. "But at a given moment I had the chance to push forward violence or stop the diabolical rhythm. We found in Moral Re-Armament a new dimension to life and to relationships between people. With this spirit a new type of diplomacy can see the light of day."

June 11, 1987

Last words of an Irish lass

ENNISKILLEN is a quiet historic town in Northern Ireland. Its local newspaper rejoices in the title *The Impartial Reporter and Farming Journal*. I have always had a liking for the ring of the town's name, perhaps because my uncle was the regimental sergeant major of its famous Royal Inniskilling Fusiliers and as a young boy I was impressed with the fancy plume and badge on his beret.

The name Enniskillen went around the world in sad circumstances at the end of 1987, because of the Irish Republican Army bomb which exploded there on Remembrance Day killing 11 Protestants at their annual war memorial service.

As bombs go and as Irish history has gone it was not the worst of outrages. But there was an element to it that somehow reached people in both Protestant and Catholic communities, in both Northern Ireland and the Republic, and in Britain, and which stirred deeper emotions than hate and revenge. The Irish Prime Minister, Charles Haughey, supported a call by the combined churches for a minute's silence throughout the Republic in memory of the bomb victims. An AP dispatch reported that the "revulsion felt throughout the island over the slaughter of innocents at prayer has forged a determination that it will never happen again."

It all had a lot to do with the demeanor on television of Gordon Wilson who had lain under the rubble with his 20-year-old daughter, Marie, and held her hand as she died. "I bear no ill will," he said the next day. He and his wife, Joan, sought not revenge but peace. "She had been screaming at me, then reassuring me," he said of Marie. " 'Daddy, I love you very much.' Those were the last words she spoke. Marie's last words were of love. It would be no way for me to remember her by having words of hatred in my mouth."

A *New York Times* correspondent wrote, "In part because of Gordon Wilson's ability to articulate the personal grief so often overlooked in political violence, the bombing is being cited and pondered more than the usual Irish violence." The AP correspondent commented, "His soft-spoken fortitude inspired Northen Irelanders on both sides of the religious divide." Indeed, Queen Elizabeth II in her Christmas message quoted Wilson and said everyone had been moved by his words.

After his TV appearance the bereaved father received 5000 letters of support from around the world. From Dublin the Lord Mayor brought books of condolence with 45,000 signatures from the Republic. The Catholic Cardinal, Thomas O'Fiaich, Primate of All Ireland, appeared on television and asked forgiveness of all the Protestants. And the Protestant Bishop whose diocese includes Enniskillen, the Rt. Rev. Brian Hannon, spoke at a memorial service in Dublin attended by 4,000 people. "May God forgive us, individually and as communities," he said, "for actions and attitudes of ours that have contributed to the violence or the anger which leads to it."

I spoke last month to the Irish Consul General in San Francisco, Brian Nason. He said that the tragedy in Enniskillen had created a backlash towards the Irish Republican

Army, and had ensured ratification by the Irish Parliament of the European Convention on Terrorism. He confirmed the increased readiness of Protestants and Catholics to understand each other's point of view. "The progress towards reconciliation is alive and well," he told me, "and a force to be reckoned with."

We will continue to read disquieting reports in our papers. But when we do let us remember the many Protestants and Catholics, who, perhaps more than ever before in history, are working quietly for a new day. And let us hope that in the years to come the long-suffering people of Northern Ireland may be able to point to Enniskillen as a turning point in their troubles.

January 22, 1988

5 On my mind

I'm starting with the man in the mirror
I'm asking him to make a change.
If you want to see the world a different place
Take a look at yourself and make a change.

Michael Jackson song

A traveler from Athens to Corinth meets another traveler on the road. "Where are you coming from?" he asks. "Corinth," he responds. "Will I like Corinth?" the first man asks. "Did you like Athens?" "No." "Well, you won't like Corinth."

Aesop's Fables

Useless Europeans

I WAS ASKED by a TV interviewer the other day what Europeans feel about America. It is, of course, an impossible question to answer. Feelings vary from country to country, from family to family, from person to person, from day to day. They are affected by age, by experience, by the prevailing mood. I, who was evacuated to this country during World War II and lived for five years with a generous American family, naturally feel differently than my uncle, an artillery officer who was shelled by mistake by his American allies.

I think the TV interviewer's question was prompted by the prevailing feeling that anti-Americanism is rampant in Europe. Only last month we read of a demonstration of 100,000 people in London against American policy. It is understandable that Americans who have done so much for Europe should sometimes feel that Europeans are less grateful than they should be. And I am sure that this is so. The London *Economist* even coined the phrase last year "the useless European" to conjure up the picture Americans were beginning to form. It predicted that the American reaction to the "useless European" would not be simply to abandon him but just to push Europe another notch downwards in America's order of priorities.

As I thought about the question I realized first that a lot of criticism of the United States is just the reaction of those who have been displaced in world leadership. A former British Member of Parliament, Woodrow Wyatt, wrote in *The Times*, "Why are we so ready to query American motives and actions? Jealousy."

And second I saw that much criticism stems from short term political disagreement with specific policies. Indeed, after listening to the way some Europeans criticize Washington, I could easily think they were Oregonians talking.

Admiral James Eberle, Director of London's Royal Institute of International Affairs, makes another point: "It is always comforting to have friends who are rich, powerful, and generous, and the Americans are certainly all three. But when your friends become too rich and too powerful, they can be very difficult to live with and to like – especially when their need to feel appreciated requires constant reinforcement."

There is another side to this question which became clear to me when I recently managed to lay my hands on a private study commissioned by the US Information Agency on the long term trends in European public opinion toward the United States. It is that Europe is perhaps not so anti-American as we have been led to believe.

The study covers France, Germany, Italy and Britain. It does indicate some erosion of respect for the United States overall and a feeling that when it comes to dealing with the Soviet Union, European and US basic interests differ. That's not surprising. For, as Lord Carrington, Secretary-General of NATO, said recently, a new generation in Britain and on the continent is not so automatically pro-US as their elders, who remember World War II, the Marshall Plan, and the origins of NATO.

But one thing is clear: in the 25 years or so these polls have been conducted, avowed anti-Americanism has never been the perspective of even as much as a quarter of the population in any of these countries. In Britain, for instance, 79% of the population voice the view that the basic interests of Britain and the US are fairly well in agreement.

A Roper poll taken a year earlier says that the descriptions Europeans typically link to life in the U.S. include guaranteed political rights, equal justice under law, religious freedom and the chances for people to get ahead. Even in the area of foreign policy the characteristics associated with the US include helping poorer countries develop, fostering human rights in other countries, and wanting agreement in reducing nuclear arms.

So it is important for Americans, while working to change what is wrong, not to underestimate what this country still represents, and to recognize that much criticism stems from the high expectations others have of this land. As writer Robin Cody put it in an article in *Northwest Magazine* about

what attracts immigrants to this country, "Behind the hype
and the hoopla, beyond the flag-waving and chest-thumping,
burns a noble idea. It survives war and depression. It endures
scandal and defeat. It shines through two centuries as the
continuing hope of the world."

Here's one European who gives thanks for America.

November 28, 1985

Twelve steps

SOME WILL KNOW THE STORY, no doubt apocryphal, of the
policeman who saw a man about to jump off the Golden
Gate Bridge. He rushed up to him to try to dissuade him.
They had a long talk – and then they both jumped. Well, a
true story of a different kind happened exactly 50 years ago
this month. One drunk got together with another drunk.
They both wanted to give up the drink. And out of their
association came the remarkable worldwide fellowship of
Alcoholics Anonymous which is today a source of hope and
support to more than a million members in over a hundred
countries. There are some 200 AA groups in the Portland
area alone.

Some local members of AA whom I have met have told
me of the similarity they perceive between the principles of
AA and those which they have heard me put forward from
Moral Re-Armament. This is not coincidence. Reading AA
literature in this past week, in particular the writings of co-
founders Bill and Bob, and Bill's wife, Lois, it is clear that
Alcoholics Anonymous has its roots in the Oxford Group,
the name by which Moral Re-Armament was earlier known.
As Lois writes, "The Oxford Group's part in AA's beginnings
can never be forgotten."

Although AA is celebrating its 50 years, to mark the meeting between New York stockbroker Bill and Ohio surgeon Dr. Bob, Bill often spoke of an earlier meeting which was also key. Rowland H., from a well-to-do Vermont family had become a hopeless drunk. He was put into the care of the world famous psychiatrist, Dr. Carl Jung, in Zurich. But after a year Jung had to tell the American that he had frankly never seen a single case recover through psychiatry where the neurosis was so severe. "Is this really the end of the line for me?" asked Rowland. "Well," replied the doctor, "there are some exceptions, a very few. Once in a while, alcoholics have had what are called vital spiritual experiences." "But," protested the patient, "I'm a religious man, and I still have faith." Jung replied, "Ordinary religious faith isn't enough. What I'm talking about is a transforming experience. I can only recommend that you place yourself in the religious atmosphere of your own choice, that you recognize your personal hopelessness, and that you cast yourself upon whatever God you think there is. It is your only way out."

Rowland found that transforming experience in the Oxford Group and the obsession to drink left him. It started a chain reaction, first to his friend Ebby, then to Ebby's friend Bill. "My doctor had given me up," Bill wrote later. "He had been obliged to tell me that I was the victim of a neurotic compulsion to drink that no amount of willpower, education, or treatment could check. I was ready for the message that was to come from my alcoholic friend Ebby." Bill began to try the ideas of the Oxford Group. He couldn't make the break immediately. But at the point of blackest depression he had ever known, lying in hospital, he cried out, "Now I'm ready to do anything to receive what my friend Ebby has." He made a frantic appeal, "If there be a God, will He show himself." "The result," in Bill's own words, "was instant, electric, beyond description. The place seemed to light up, blinding white. I knew only ecstasy, and seemed on a mountain. A great wind blew, enveloping and penetrating me. To me it was not of air, but of Spirit. Blazing, there came a tremendous thought, 'You're a free man.' " And Bill never touched another drop.

That was December 1934. Five months later he carried the message to Dr. Bob. All three found at Oxford Group meetings a kind of enthusiasm and friendship which Bill described as "manna from Heaven." On the platform and off men and women, young and old, told how their lives had been transformed. "Little was heard of theology," wrote Bill in *Pass It On*, "but we heard plenty of absolute honesty, purity, unselfishness and love. They were talking about God-centeredness versus self-centeredness. The basic principles which the Oxford Groupers had taught were ancient and universal ones, the common property of mankind – the earlier AA got its ideas of self-examination, acknowledgement of character defects, restitution for harm done, and working with others straight from the Oxford Groups."

Both Bob and Bill felt their call was not, as they put it, with the Oxford Group to save the world, but to sober up alcoholics. They gradually worked out the ideas of AA as we know them today, with its principle of anonymity and a freedom from rules. The only requirement for membership is a desire to stop drinking. There are no dues, nor is AA allied to any other group or engaging in any causes or controversy. Though there are now two related fellowships to help relatives of alcoholics, Al-Anon Family Groups and Alateen for teenagers who have alcoholic parents.

At the heart of Alchoholics Anonymous is the experience of the Twelve Steps.

1. We admitted we were powerless over alcohol – that our lives had become unmanageable.

2. Came to believe that a Power greater than ourselves could restore us to sanity.

3. Made a decision to turn our will and our lives over to the care of God as we understood Him.

4. Made a searching and fearless moral inventory of ourselves.

5. Admitted to God, to ourselves, and to another human being the exact nature of our wrongs.

6. Were entirely ready to have God remove all these defects of character.

7. Humbly asked Him to remove our shortcomings.

8. Made a list of all persons we had harmed, and became willing to make amends to them all.

9. Made direct amends to such people wherever possible, except when to do so would injure them or others.

10. Continued to take personal inventory and when we were wrong promptly admitted it.

11. Sought through prayer and meditation to improve our conscious contact with God, as we understood Him, praying only for knowledge of His will for us and the power to carry that out.

12. Having had a spiritual awakening as the result of these steps we tried to carry this message to alcoholics, and to practice these principles in all our affairs.

Not a bad check list for any of us, drunk or sober.

June 20, 1985

Shooting the cabinet

A KNOWLEDGEABLE South African told me the other day that if you lined up the South African cabinet against a wall and gave them the chance to save their lives by denying Christ, they would to a man prefer to be shot.

I don't know if that is an exaggeration. I think from my experience of Afrikaaners that it is not. They are men and women of deep faith and on a personal level often treat those around them, whatever their race, very considerately.

This makes it all the sadder that they seem to have a blind spot when it comes to the wider application of Christian teaching.

The tragedy and the hope in South Africa in a way both reside in the Christian faith. The tragedy is that Christians have for so long treated others in a sub-Christian fashion, and have even enshrined Christianity and apartheid in the same constitution. The hope is that the vast majority of all races still claim to be Christians and therefore presumably believe in the power of God to change human lives and intervene through changed lives in the governance of the state, in the power of prayer, and above all, at this late hour, in the power of forgiveness.

Sometimes we are not aware of the tremendous rethinking going on among people of faith in South Africa – even at the heart of the Dutch Reformed Church which claims 60% of the white community. Two years ago 148 ministers of that church issued an open letter, and with considerable courage laid their convictions on the line. They said, "A social order which alienates the different sections of the South African population from one another is unacceptable. The laws which have become symbols of this alienation, among those concerning mixed marriages, race classification, and group areas cannot be defended scripturally." In the statement they went on to outline actions which could not be reconciled with biblical demands for justice and human dignity. They added, "We confess to our deepest guilt before God that we have also failed to manifest adequately the unity of the Church of Christ in our lives and that we too have contributed to many of the social evils we have identified."

In another change of direction the Western Cape Synod of the Dutch Reformed Church disassociated itself from any attempt to present separate development as if it were laid down by the Bible. This was the same Synod which in 1936 asked the then government to introduce the policy of apartheid.

This fall there have been some significant developments which have received scant coverage in our papers. For instance, in September 400 Christian leaders representing 47 denominations met at a National Initiative for Reconciliation. The group included people who were theologically poles apart and yet talked together, as one observer commented, in an extraordinary unity. It was a time when many of the white delegates had the chance to learn firsthand of the suffering in other communites. As one commentator put it, "It took the wraps off a mutilated black South Africa about which the whites are in general utterly ignorant."

No list of delegates was published but amongst them were the heads of the Anglican, Catholic, Presbyterian and Methodist churches, and although the Dutch Reformed Church did not appoint formal representatives it sent 50 senior delegates who made up the biggest group of all.

At the end the leaders issued a Statement of Affirmation which was accepted by all but six delegates, and which committed them both to an ongoing process of reconciliation, and to work for concrete changes in South African society. "We found an astonishing measure of unity where formerly we knew little but division," they stated. "We believe the spirit of God is urging us and the whole South African church in new and more determined ways to prepare people for living in a changed and totally non-racial land."

Out of this three-day gathering came the idea for a national day of repentance, mourning, and prayer for "those sinful aspects of our national life which have led us to the present crisis," and for a delegation to visit the South African President, urging him to take practical steps, including the ending of the Emergency, the release of detainees, and the elimination of all legislated discrimination.

To outside observers such changes may not seem all that dramatic, but for a deeply religious people they are pivotal. Botha, Buthelezi, Tutu, Boesak — their common ground is not only that they are South African but that they are also Christian. And the key question is whether the new thinking and living among Christians can spread fast enough and deep enough. As author Alan Paton, who opened the Reconciliation meeting, said, quoting Proverbs, "Hope deferred makes the heart sick."

To come back to my South African friend's word at the beginning, I have a feeling that if the South African cabinet took Christ's claims seriously and lived them in their fullest dimension, then no one would get shot.

November 21, 1985

Holy gamble

I BELIEVE that God can speak to Oral Roberts as specifically as he can to me and you.

I accept that the preacher believes God said he would "call him home to heaven" if four and a half million dollars were not raised by March 31.

I have trouble accepting, however, that such a profound matter should have been divulged to the public at large, that it is right, to use modern jargon, to lay such a potential guilt trip on others.

A far greater, and to my mind, more authentic road of faith would have been for Roberts, if he received this confidence from God, to have said nothing about it.

It is true that God's ways are not our ways, and as this is certainly not our way, it could be God's way. It might be argued that by making what to many is an outrageous suggestion Roberts has been given many more secular pulpits, like ABC's "Good Morning America" and the "Larry King Show," from which to proclaim God's message. And it takes considerable courage to be prepared to go out on such a spiritual limb.

On the other hand, it is very easy for those of us of faith to move beyond proclaiming the gospel in God's way to pressurizing people to go along with our way. Where God guides, he provides; that is the undeniable experience of millions of people over the years. But if that is the case we Christians have to be sure that we really are being guided by God. When hard sell becomes the order of the day, it can be that ambition has drowned out the still, small voice.

I do not believe, as Richard Roberts, Oral's son, says, that the center of the controversy is the theological question whether God speaks directly to people today or not. It is much more whether God's words, real or imagined, should be used in this way as a spiritual club to achieve a worldly aim.

I do not begrudge money for Oral Roberts' medical missions. I admire the way his students chip in their dollars.

I certainly do not wish for his demise. I do not even wish these words to be construed as singling him out for criticism. It is just that this incident has encouraged me to express a dormant concern about some emphases on the part of some of those in what is called the electronic church.

Frankly, I would rather see people giving money in response to public appeals by preachers than falling for advertisements for secular products they don't really need. God does something in the heart of a giver that is immeasurable and healthy. At the same time I worry about the effect of pressure, humanly orchestrated spiritual pressure, on those who can ill afford to part with their money.

I worry most about what message we Christians are communicating about Christ and his way for the world, and fear that preoccupation with the bizarre could turn away millions, or inoculate them against the real thing. It is, after all, human abuses of God's ability to speak which through history have strengthened the hand of those who say that he doesn't. I fear that Oral Robert's pronouncement may come into that category.

Many of us who can attest to the experience of God speaking know that the validity of such "guidance" has to be carefully tested against the scrutiny both of the Bible and of wise Christian fellowship. It is hardly scriptural to see death as an act of divine punishment and God as a dealer; and a man at the head of a Christian organization may need a wider circle of outside friends as well as subordinates with whom to consult on matters as important as this.

God, we are told, is always available, but anyone who has made a daily discipline of listening for direction knows that it is sometimes hard to recognize his voice and that we have to constantly guard against self-delusion.

Certainly, once he has spoken we have to obey promptly, and move boldly in faith. But our actions have always to be tempered with a considerable measure of humility and one certainty: we may be wrong.

Oral Robert's "holy gamble" is, I understand, attracting bookmakers' odds. Will he or will he not be able to raise the money to keep himself alive? He now says he expects to live beyond March 31. The deadline has, so to speak, been lifted. But I'd be wary of any story about him that you read on April Fool's day.

February 26, 1987

Christians kill Christ

I DON'T THINK I have any prejudice against Jewish people or ever have had. At the age of 12 I wrote an essay in a national competition for a paper in this country about prejudice, and I can remember specifically decrying anti-semitic language. It got an honorable mention and, curiously, when I recently saw a clipping about it I noted that the winner had been a girl from St. Helen's Hall, Portland.

I have never understood the mentality of those who hold against Jews the killing of Christ, a Jew whom I have given my life to follow. I prefer the view of a great English journalist and Christian, Peter Howard. In his preface to *Mr. Brown Comes Down the Hill*, a play about how Christ might be treated if he came back to earth today, Howard writes, "The real Christ-killers were supporters of Christ – snobs who came by night but turned aside in the daylight, a mob which cheered when things were going well and jeered when they went badly, close friends and supporters who ratted when enemies came to arrest Christ and take him away."

I realize, however, that I have felt that the effort on the part of some Jews to keep the Holocaust alive and to track down every possible wartime oppressor of Jews, was excessive, and indeed likely to be counterproductive, and that in so feeling I have been out of step with most Jews. I have wished that more Jews would stress forgiveness of their erstwhile enemies, as some did soon after the war.

It has become clear to me recently however that I have not lived enough into the history of the Jews, and why they feel as they do. That must be a prerequisite of any expectation of forgiveness. I have not seriously given thought to how much we Christians have contributed to the feeling of persecution. As Peter Howard writes in that same preface, "Counting up all the massacres, all the miseries, all the degradations of the human spirit and heart in the last 2000 years, it is probable that Christians have persecuted Jews as brutally as did Hitler." The reason, according to Howard, is a guilty conscience. "For it is the Christians who continue to kill Christ," he writes.

As Passover approaches it might be appropriate for those of us who call ourselves Christians to think more about this issue. It might be a good moment, too, to share the content of a remarkable speech which I had occasion to read recently. It was a plenary address given at the December meeting of the American Psychoanalytical Association at the Waldorf-Astoria Hotel in New York by Joseph V. Montville, Research Director of the Center for the Study of Foreign Affairs at the Foreign Service Institute of the State Department. The title was "Psychoanalytic Enlightenment and the Greening of Diplomacy."

Montville, a career diplomat but speaking in a private capacity, described in this address the way psychoanalysis had helped him as a political analyst and a student of conflict resolution. He talked of the victimization which leads to groups feeling unrelieved, conscious anxiety about threats to their existence. He gave examples in the contemporary scene, ranging from the Basques in Spain who fear loss of language, culture and identity through pressure for assimilation into Spanish society, to Israelis' fears of a mass of hostile Arabs surrounding them and waiting for just the right moment to push them into the sea. And he added, after the latter example, "As a doubly wrenching twist of cruel fate, Israelis also fear that the Gentile – really the Christian – world would watch passively, while feigning shocked outrage, as the Arabs completed the "final solution" to the "Jewish problem."

This Foreign Service officer said that skeptics could be excused if they doubted the day would come when political leaders would acknowledge and accept responsiblity for their, or their predecessors, oppression of their victims. But over the past 40 years there had been examples where victims and oppressors had been able to reestablish relations on a different basis. He cited experiences between France and Germany, between Japan and the United States, between Japan and her Southeast Asian neighbors, between blacks and whites in Zimbabwe, and even embryo relations now being built between Protestants and Catholics in Northern Ireland, and between Israelis, Palestinians and Egyptians.

But in many ways the most significant, and certainly as far as those present were concerned the most moving, part of his address was his outline of the terrible things done over centuries to Jews in the very name of Christ, creating what he called "the most painful and perhaps the most dangerous of historic grievances, that is of Jews against Gentiles, against Christians." And then his own personal readiness to face his responsibility as a Christian.

He ended his address with the words, "I want to take advantage of this public occasion to ask as a private, individual Christian, the forgiveness of the Jewish people for the hurts inflicted on them by Christendom. I ask to be permitted to mourn Jewish losses with Jews, and then work in brotherly alliance with Jews and Arabs to mourn unjust hurts suffered by some Arabs as Jews fleeing Christian brutality in Europe established a homeland in Palestine and ultimately the State of Israel. And I ask to work with Jews and Arabs to establish a relationship which assures a secure and just future for them and their children."

April 9, 1987

No punishment from God

WHAT A REVOLUTION we've seen in our eating habits. Who would have imagined a few years back that we would now eagerly be consuming 100% milk-free milk, or litespread instead of butter, nutrasweet instead of sugar, herbs instead of salt, sizzlean instead of bacon? Who had ever heard of cholesterol? It's amazing what the fear of death through heart disease has done to us.

What a revolution, too, in our smoking habits, with ordinances being adopted everywhere to prevent puffing in public transport, in the workplace, in restaurants, and concern about the effect of smoking on non-smokers. It's amazing what fear of death through cancer has done.

American attitudes can be changed dramatically and quickly, given sufficient reason.

Now, you'd have to be blind or deaf or living in another world not to have noted through the massive State advertising campaign that AIDS is a killer. Could it be then, that AIDS, like cholesterol and cancer, is destined to provoke a life style change for Americans?

To be frank, any other approaches, as scientific and sophisticated and liberated as they may sound, are not going to touch the core of the problem. Purer livers are more reliable than safer sex.

The AIDS epidemic is a catastrophic consequence of the sexual revolution. Twenty-five years ago a doctor friend of mine in Britain got into trouble for suggesting that extramarital intercourse was medically dangerous. Today his words look prophetic. For what was once only sinful is now suicidal. Paul Johnson, the noted British historian, writes, "The truth is, the only sensible advice the government can give the public can be summed up in six words: chastity before marriage, fidelity within it. But that would be to endorse traditional Judeo-Christian morality, and so is automatically ruled out."

But it is not ruled out for religious leaders. In Britain some have been outspoken. Cardinal Basil Hume of

Westminster says, "Even in the short term a moral reawakening is society's best hope." The Chief Rabbi of the Commonwealth, Sir Immanual Jakobiwits, writes, "Nothing short of a moral revolution will in time contain the scourge. The Jewish experience demonstrates that only spiritual power is invincible as a shield against lust." The Archbishop of York, Dr. John Hapgood, noting the emptiness of a culture that has thrown away restraint, says, "The risk of AIDS reinforces the wisdom of such Christian principles as chastity and fidelity." And the editor of the *Islamic World Review*, Fathi Osman, noting the words of these Christian and Jewish leaders, writes, "The AIDS epidemic is an opportunity to map out the exclusive ground shared by all believers in One God."

None of these men sees AIDS as a punishment from God, but rather as a proof that God's laws cannot be flouted with impunity. They would encourage compassion for the sufferer, and acknowledge that we all bear responsiblity for the moral disarray of society and the breakdown of family life. Their words give me hope that the fear of death may in this area, too, lead to new life, that churches may recover their moral authority, that purity and restraint could become as fashionable as fat-free diets, and that, as A. M. Rosenthal of the *New York Times* writes, "Out of the peril of the plague could arise a strong new American ethic of sexual responsibility." For after all, religious leaders are surely not meant to move with the times but to change them. "In purer lives thy service find."

December 4, 1987

Good on 'ya, mate

"IF AMERICA was founded by idealists seeking to fulfil their ideals, Australia was founded by convicts serving out their convictions." So writes an Australian friend of mine. Australian history is closely linked with American independence. Indeed, Allan Griffith, an Australian foreign policy expert, says that in helping colonize Australia with convicts and marine guards, Britain's Royal Navy entertained a secret wish. Until 1776, North America's stand of Douglas fir trees had provided the Navy with masts for its ships. But with British rule in America gone, he says, it hoped that Australia's Norfolk Island pines would fill the gap.

For Australians to be so forthcoming about their roots – "My ancestors were picked by the best judges in England," one of them jokes – is a new phenomenon. This openness was given a fillip last year by the publication of Robert Hughes', *The Fatal Shore* (Knopf), which in graphic detail, almost to the point of overkill, depicts the sufferings of the early penal colony. Now this year, of course, the whole nation in its Bicentenary bash is focussing on this past.

Americans over recent years have become increasingly aware of Australia, particularly through its films and miniseries, and its sporting prowess and Oregonian links are growing.

Australia is nearly as large as the United States but has only 16 million inhabitants. Thanks to its immigration policies since World War II, and to a generous welcome to refugees – Australia accepted more Indo-Chinese per head of population than any other country – today's Australians come from 120 countries. And only a small minority would be able to find a convict ancestor – hence the motto of the Bicentenary: "Living Together."

Billions of dollars are being spent down under on some 50,000 events around the continent. These include the retracing of the epic voyage of convicts from England, the Tall Ships race from Hobart, the Brisbane World Expo 88 which will be opened by Queen Elizabeth, and a comprehensive Bicentennial Arts Program. There will be the world's largest dance (20,000 in a woolshed) and the creation of the world's largest fruit salad, and, of course, the World Boomerang Throwing Cup. Canberra will be the starting point for the Around Australia relay race, which will involve 16,000 runners on a 10,870 mile course and end at the capital in December.

There is one discordant note. Aboriginal activists are observing a year of mourning for what they see as a celebration of the occupation of their land. On New Year's day they threw wreaths on the beach where British explorer Capt. James Cook landed in 1770, eighteen years before the first colonists. Aborigines make up one percent of the population.

Many descendants of the first European colonists have called for the Bicentenary to be an occasion for national reconciliation. Michael Brown writes in *For A Change*, "As we mark our Bicentenary we cannot fail, by any scale of objectivity, to honor the 200 bicentenaries of Aboriginal occupancy of this land – which by most scientific count goes back beyond 40,000 years."

Brown's conviction comes from discovering in his own family's past the "skeleton" of a great great uncle who in 1851 was killed by Aboriginals, and an unknown number of "skeletons" of Aboriginals who were shot down in revenge without understanding or trial. "Whenever I have simply expressed to an Aboriginal my repentance for the sins of my fathers, and for my own indifference over years," he says, "I have found an amazing response – a bond of forgiveness and understanding."

This Australian writer sees the Bicentenary as a time for his countrymen and women neither to idolize the myths of the Aussie background and character nor to damn themselves with past mistakes. "But," as he writes, "through baring our souls over what is plainly wrong amongst us, and taking some risks in an effort to reshape our own attitudes and living, we might find real growth towards maturity in national character."

Good on'ya, mate. Perhaps there's a place, too, for a few

pommies to make amends. If we English put right some
present attitudes and past actions, we might not get a recurrence of the little Australian girl bursting into tears when she
heard she was to go to England. "What's the trouble?" she
was asked. "I don't want to go to England," she replied,
"because that's where all the convicts come from."

January 14, 1988

Spiritual interdependence

I READ two news items this past week which on the surface,
and I fear beneath the surface, were contradictory.

The first was the announcement in *The Oregonian* of the
award of the Templeton Prize for progress in religion to a
Muslim leader, Inamullah Khan, who is a founder and Secretary-General of the World Muslim Congress.

The Templeton, a sort of Nobel prize in the field of
religion, has been awarded over the years to thirteen Christians, one Hindu and one Buddhist. Inamullah Khan was
cited for his "tireless work as a coordinator for peace
between Muslims, Christians and Jews."

The second item was a paragraph in the latest issue of
US News and World Report reporting on the annual prayer
breakfast in Washington DC last month. Apparently Prince
Bandar, Saudi Arabia's Ambassador to the United States,
was one of the speakers at the breakfast and quoted from
the Koran. A leader of the National Association of Evangeli-
cals is reported as saying, "The inside word is that this will
not happen again. The focus of the National Prayer Breakfast
has always been on the Bible, reflecting America's historic
background. That is the way it should be."

The unnamed leader quoting the unnamed insider is

entitled to his or her opinion, but I doubt very much that it represents the spirit of those who organize those breakfasts. It does, however, underline the need for both vision and caution in the matter of relations between religions. These relations are supremely important, for the future of the world may depend on the way in which the people of faith stand together. Indeed, Inamullah Khan, welcoming the Pope to Karachi, said, "Between us Muslims and Christians we represent nearly 50% of the world's population. Given genuine goodwill and understanding, our two communities can be a source of real peace on the basis of justice the world over."

We have a lot to learn about the Muslim faith – and unlearn. One scholar has pointed out that until 1955 ninety-five percent of the books published on Islam in the West were written by Western orientalists. Imagine how we would feel if we discovered that 95% of the books about Christianity had been written by Muslim scholars! It might make those of us who claim to be Christian a little less strident if we applied to ourselves the perspective of a great Buddhist scholar I once heard speak to an American audience. "Do you know why I am a Buddhist?" he asked. We waited for the learned answer. "I am a Buddhist because I was born in Sri Lanka." It is probably good for those of us who are Episcopalians to realize, too, that we are outnumbered in the United States by Muslims, who now have 600 Mosques.

Christians and Muslims probably have more that unites them than divides them. We believe in one God, we have a common source of morality beginning in the Ten Commandments, a common dependence on God's grace and pardon, a common belief in a day of judgment, and underlying it all the common foundation of surrender to God's will.

My experience in many parts of the world leads me to the conclusion that in countries where other faiths are predominant people do not basically object to Christians who live their faith. What has more often alienated them is Christians who don't, or countries who claim to be Christian but whose policies seem to contradict that claim.

The leader of my church, Dr. Robert Runcie, Archbishop

of Canterbury, gave a remarkable lecture after a visit to India. He came back with the conviction that our world desperately needed a new and larger vision of unity which transcends our differences. He said that we needed both the courage and humility to recognize the work of the spirit among us in other faiths, and to acknowledge religious diversity as a rich spiritual resource. "It takes humility and sincerity," he went on, "to concede that there is a certain incompleteness in each of our traditions."

The life, suffering, death, and resurrection of Jesus Christ would, for Christians, he said, always remain the primary source of knowledge and truth about God. The central message of the Christian gospel was not negotiable. "Nonetheless, Christians recognize," he said, "that other faiths reveal other aspects of God which may enrich and enlarge our Christian understanding."

We had to move beyond monologue to dialogue. "Interfaith dialogue can help to remove barriers between us by creating conditions for greater community and fellowship," he said. "This will mean that some claims about the exclusiveness of the Church have to be renounced, but also that past and present prejudices about other religions have to be overcome, and ignorance and contempt actively resisted."

True dialogue, he said, "can help us recognize that faiths other than our own are genuine mansions of the Spirit with many rooms to be discovered, rather than solitary fortresses to be attacked."

In that spirit we can welcome awards to non-Christians for progress in religion, and learn from their faith – even over breakfast.

March 10, 1988

An honest coach

DON'T BELIEVE everything you read in the papers or see on television. You often hear that said. But a more accurate truth would be: don't believe that what you read in the papers or see on television is everything. The nature of news is such that it revels in the new, the different, the odd, the bizarre, the unusual – with the result that we get a view of only part of our world, and sometimes a skewed one at that.

A man I was sitting next to at lunch last week, who happened to be a fireman, said to me, "You have to turn half a dozen pages before you find anything positive, and on television it's death, destruction, pestilence, disease." He exaggerates, but he would have a fellow feeling with a lady who, when she heard I was a journalist, said, "Oh, I haven't subscribed to a newspaper in months and I feel so much better. It's like, when I gave up smoking."

If it's news about our own community we can evaluate what we read and see by our own experience. We realize, for instance, that a blaze in one house in one suburb doesn't mean our whole city's on fire. But when a story is about some distant part of the world we know nothing about, we have no protective filter. I once went into a travel agency and saw a map of Ireland with a line through it and the words written across the whole island, "state of war." It was untrue, and unfair to the tourist industry of the country, north and south.

This applies equally to foreigners looking at the United States. If their only exposure to this country is "Dallas" or "Miami Vice," or news of politicians' peccadilloes or of educational inadequacies or of evangelical falls from grace, they don't know the big heart of America. Unfortunately, this focus on the negative means that too many Americans are more conscious of anti-Americanism than of the deep wells of gratitude millions around the world have for this land, and are more aware of this country's blemishes than of the hope she still represents for the future of our planet.

An English friend, John Lester, was in the United States

this summer when the TV screens were monopolized by Ollie North and John Poindexter, and Jim and Tammy Bakker, and suchlike un-American originals. He might have been forgiven, he says, for assuming that lying was endemic in the United States.

Then suddenly his attention was caught by a different story. It was about a small college basketball team which had against all odds become league champions. The town celebrated and feted their coach. A few weeks later, however, the coach discovered that in one match of the many played a substitute had come on who did not have the number of grades required for eligibility. He had been on court only two minutes. This coach went to the authorities and told them the truth, and as a result the shield was given to another team.

The story was the more poignant, my friend writes, because the coach was a black man in a largely white neighborhood. When asked why he did it, the coach replied simply that to have done anything else would have been dishonest. The townspeople were disappointed but registered almost total support for the integrity of the coach. As John writes, "It demonstrates the foolishness of judging a country by the news story that happens to be uppermost."

A simple step of honesty by one comparatively unknown American has outweighed for my friend all the millions of words and hours of pictures devoted to supposedly more important people and events.

That's the kind of America I give thanks for, too, at this time. And, he saw it on television.

November 27, 1987

6 Americana

"Everybody can be great. Because anybody can serve. You don't have to have a college degree to serve. You don't have to make your subject and verb agree to serve. You don't have to know about Plato and Aristotle to serve. You don't have to know Einstein's Theory of Relativity to serve. You don't have to know the second Theory of Thermodynamics to serve. You only need a heart full of grace, a soul generated by love."

Martin Luther King, Jr.

Small Japanese boy on first visit to United States: "Look, they have McDonalds here too."

America, America!
God mend thine every flaw,
Confirm thy soul in self-control,
Thy liberty in law.

America The Beautiful

My soul is a strange companion

ONCE YOU'D MET John Coleman, you didn't forget him. His graphic turn of phrase, his cheery disposition, his overweight frame, were tribute to a black man who had allowed his Christian commitment to override the poverty, bitterness and, as he would admit, the drunkenness of his past.

People in Portland remember his visit a few years back and his challenging words. "White folk," he told us, "are walking around with a social disease of guilt, and black folk are walking around with a social disease of bitterness. The white man has got to repent, but the black man has got to forgive."

John Coleman, of Richmond, Virginia, died of a heart attack a couple of months back, and it is perhaps appropriate in Black History Month to say a word about a man who was described by the *Richmond Times-Dispatch* as "a black community activist whose life's work was to heal relationships, particularly those between the races."

More than a thousand people, including a Catholic bishop, three Episcopal bishops, and a representative of the Episcopal Church's presiding bishop, attended his funeral, and he is the first black to be buried in what had been the city's exclusively white Hollywood Cemetery. The words which he asked to be inscribed on his tombstone read: "Here lies a man who gave his coat and a loaf of bread to a man who needed it."

John grew up in a segregated city, was a high school dropout, worked as a sailor and a postal clerk, and studied sociology. Along the way he developed into an embittered alcoholic. But after a remarkable turnaround, which included getting an MA without having an undergraduate degree, and teaching for four years at the University of Richmond, he became a spokesman for Christian community, and in the words of Virginia Bishop Peter Lee "embodied reconciliation." "If you seek his memorial, look around you today," said Lee. "He fought racism, but he did it with love. He fought poverty, yet he engendered hope. He lived to make this a place of many mansions, with room for anyone."

Coleman was a deeply spiritual being. "I sit at the feet of the Lord as a total surrender of my incomplete life," he once wrote. "I pray often. Sometimes I keep quiet and listen to the Lord. In a quiet moment, I heard him say that before I can minister in his name I must walk his walk. I must take on his ways – and be led by his spirit."

He was also intensely practical, particularly in dealing with the pressures from all who came to him for help. His job, he said, was to respond to the need presented to him, not to be a judge of character, a mind reader, or a trade-off master. But sometimes he had to say, "No." "Giving a can of beans, a worn coat, or two dollars is easy, when they are available. My greatest struggle during these encounters is to keep myself together, so that I will be around to feed the next herd of sheep." A fellow seminarian said of Coleman, "He taught me to take the bus, not the plane; to stay at the YMCA, not the Hilton; to sit on the wall of the seminary and talk to those going by."

The black social worker faced criticism with a light touch. He recalled speaking at an affluent white church. When he had finished a man came up to him and, feeling his three-piece, blue-striped suit, said, "This doesn't look like poverty to me, John." "What else did I speak about besides poverty?" responded Coleman. "The goodness of God," the man said. "Well," said Coleman, "this suit is an example of God's goodness to one of his servants."

In a book of his sayings, *My Soul is a Strange Companion*, Coleman wrote, "It's difficult to shift gears from feeling like a victim, to taking some responsibility for my own life. I have discovered that I am a valuable human being. Now I refuse the role of being worthless. A failure is a failure – and that's not good. But my self-worth is not any less because I fail sometimes. Reality is not always kind to me. When I am forced to face it, I sometimes find out I have something inside of me I didn't know I had."

A recent video, *The Courage to Change*, about the work of Richmond citizens to break down barriers in the

community, featured John Coleman's work as Director of
the Peter Paul Development Center. Located in one of the
city's most deprived areas, it is a haven for the young and
the elderly, where he tried to instill a sense of self-respect
and of belonging to a community of all God's people. In the
video he says, "If you want to be a bridge, you have to be
prepared to be walked on."

The manner of John Coleman's death was a commentary
on his life's work. He had just been talking to young people
and their parents at the historic St. Paul's Episcopal Church.
He was on his way to St. Peter's Episcopal Church where he
was to give the sermon to his fellow parishioners. He died
in the middle of the Martin Luther King Bridge, which
connects the thriving business center to his own depressed
East End, a connection he strove to develop.

"All I'm trying to do," he once said in his modest way,
"is to plant a seed and hope that when John Coleman's not
around, somebody will sprinkle a little water on it."

February 4, 1988

Not a spark of genius

WHEN an Indian friend of mine came here as a young, rather
awestruck, immigrant many years ago, he was asked at his
port of entry by the immigration officer, "Do you know
anybody in this country?" Not knowing the difference
between *know* and *know of*, he blurted out triumphantly,
"I know two people, George Washington and Abraham
Lincoln."

An African ambassador who visited Portland a while
back said that his people drew inspiration from Abraham
Lincoln. A Nationalist Chinese ambassador told me he had

founded a Lincoln Society in Taiwan. There is an attractive-
ness to the life of the sixteenth president that has inspired
foreigners as it has Americans. The great Russian, Leo
Tolstoy, said when Lincoln died that among all the heroes
and statesmen of history he was "the only real giant." And
surely the more we emulate Lincoln's example today, the
more this country will continue to exert an influence for
good in the world – even on Tolstoy's descendants.

Unlike many whose stature seems to diminish over the
years, or whose achievements are downgraded by hindsight,
Lincoln's greatness seems to grow. It is hard to believe that
in his own time the *Baltimore Sun* wrote, "We do not believe
the Presidency can ever be more degraded by any of his
successors than it has been by him." Or that Henry Ward
Beecher, the most famous preacher of the day, said, "Not a
spark of genius has he; not an element of leadership."

Lincoln was almost turned out of office by the peace
movement of the day, and his Gettysburg Address was
dismissed by the London *Times* with the comment that it
would be hard to produce anything more dull and
commonplace.

The bold strokes of Lincoln's life are as familiar to Americans as the penny and the $5 bill that carry his likeness, and
the words of some of his immortal speeches. The Lincoln
Memorial must be one of the most inspirational shrines in
the world. He is honored for having preserved the Union.

Columnist William Safire believes we miss the point,
however, if we do not go beyond that recognition to an
understanding that in being willing to go to war to uphold
majority rule Lincoln preserved democracy. "We are a super-
power today," he writes, "not because we are 50 states, but
because we are a democracy. We are a democracy, and the
last best hope of Earth, because we have enshrined majority
rule. That is the difference Lincoln made."

It is not always remembered how much Lincoln had to
contend with adversity. He had to cope with sickness and
depression, with the deaths of his mother, when he was nine,
and later his sister, two sons, and his first fiancée; he also
dealt with calumny and ridicule, with the need to go to war

and with a cabinet that opposed him and a commanding general who predicted defeat. Yet he responded with a breadth of vision and generosity that is astounding and which has left us with a legacy of stories about him. His humanity, humility, and sense of humor helped him at difficult hours. When someone made fun of his appearance, he said, "The Lord prefers common-looking people; that is the reason he made so many of them." When he felt he was wrong, he apologized. About one campaign he wrote to General Grant, "I wish to make the personal acknowledgement that you were right and I was wrong."

It was, it is clear, a faith in a divine purpose that sustained him. His advance in faith through the years was as marked as his progression from rude cabin to the White House. He never completed a year of schooling, but was to pen some of the most lasting and memorable political and spiritual truths of all time. When he became president he evoked the example of his predecessor George Washington: "I cannot succeed without the same divine aid which sustained him and on that same Almighty Being I place my reliance for support." In the National Cathedral there is a statue of the President, appropriately, on his knees.

Lincoln acquired in office the attributes that later generations were to revere. Jim Wright, Speaker of the House of Representatives, characterizes them as those set forth by Christ in the Beatitudes. He was poor; he mourned; he hungered and thirsted for righteousness; he was meek; he was merciful; he was a peacemaker. When the war was finally over there were no humiliating ceremonies of capitulation. There was to be no vengeance. The terms of the surrender were remarkably generous and gentle. Why? Because Lincoln, just hours before his assassination, had personally dictated them.

Once, when a clergyman said to Lincoln, "The Lord is on our side," Lincoln responded, "I don't agree with you." After a pause the President said, in words which are a challenge to us today, and well sum up his approach, "I am not at all concerned about that, for I know that the Lord is always on the side of the right. But it is my constant anxiety and prayer that I and this nation should be on the Lord's side."

February 12, 1987

Sticking your neck out

SOME OF US are by nature tortoises, some greyhounds, some rabbits, some wolves, some occasionally ostriches. Too many are sheep. Some lunch with lions while others eat with elks. Some are hawks and some are doves. In Oregon you will even find more than a few of us who are ducks. But I have friends who are looking for giraffes.

Let me explain. John Graham and Ann Medlock, husband and wife, are directing from an island in Puget Sound what they call the Giraffe Project. They want to honor people who stick their necks out for the common good. And what started less than two years ago as a small initiative with radio spots, has mushroomed into a program that is reaching into business and TV and even the White House. Their ambition is nothing less than to change the nature of politics.

Ann says that some of us get a distorted view of the world from the news media. The Giraffe Project grew out of their belief that traditional journalism focuses on the down side of human events to a degree that is out of proportion, and that people badly need to be exposed to news about good things that good people are doing.

John says that people can choose either to be captives of history or to make a difference. "Too many whine about things," he says, "but when push comes to shove they don't do anything about it." "Giraffes," he explains, "act out of caring; they may well rock the boat but not just to make trouble. They are devoted to making things better, not just more exciting. Their actions are ultimately healing, not divisive."

"No strategy for change works," he maintains, "unless you make the commitment to have your own life become the blueprint for the lifestyle you want to promote in others."

John believes that his fifteen years in the foreign service mean that he cannot be dismissed as an idealist. He was in Libya during the revolution that brought Gaddafi to power, and in Vietnam during the war; he has headed the section for African and Non-Aligned Affairs with the US Mission at the UN, and is a graduate of the government's Interservice Nuclear Weapons School. He also has a BA from Harvard and an MA from Stanford.

Ann has worked in presidential and gubernatorial campaigns, taught in the Congo, been editor of *Vietnam Press*, speechwriter for the Aga Khan, and Editor-in-chief of the Children's Express News Service.

When Ann and John first met in New York City, they talked over their goals, and discovered they both wanted to make a positive difference in the state of the world. "We were romantically involved before merging our professional lives," John told me. But they soon realized that their two backgrounds meant they could accomplish what they were trying to do more effectively together than separately. "I'm a knee jerk liberal," says Ann, "and he's a knee jerk conservative, so we balance each other out."

The Giraffe Project began with a media campaign on 235 radio stations. That is now more than doubling to 500 and the couple are also negotiating with companies who could do TV spots. These radio spots tell of "giraffes" they have identified, people acting with extraordinary courage and compassion. Well-known personalities give their services to record the commentaries, for instance John Denver, who says, "We think there's a risk-taker in all of us wanting to get out."

John's Political Effectiveness Seminars have now become Giraffe Workshops for teaching the practical skills needed to tackle tough challenges. A Schools Program has been developed, led by former Peace Corps volunteer Carola Wilder and all sorts of "Giraffernalia" are being distributed, including Giraffe mugs, T-shirts, pins and business cards. It is financed by a growing number of foundations, individuals and members.

Giraffes who are featured in radio and TV spots may be rich or poor, young or old, liberal or conservative. Examples include: two cops from Fort Apache who started a boxing program that now involves 300 kids and is helping reduce crime; a North Carolina housewife who gave emergency shelter for 23 refugee orphans; and a waitress who braved threats of violence to stop toxic waste dumping in her Tennessee community. Recently John and Ann had a call from the White House asking if they knew any young giraffes. Within days Petra Mastenbroek, who had started a no-drugs campaign in her Seattle school, was in the White House rose garden to receive a special commendation from the President.

John and Ann wish to hear from anyone who would like to nominate giraffes, people who have taken social, physical, or financial risk for the common good. The couple has established a giraffe hotline at 800 344–TALL. "You're only a giraffe when you go beyond your job description," they say. And they add, "Please don't send stories of dare-devil racing drivers or hang gliders, and, though we understand the feelings involved, please don't nominate 'my wife Joan for putting up with me all these years.' "

December 5, 1985

Tongue in cheekbone

FRIENDSHIP is a great blessing in life. Some people have few friends, some many. And, as Aristotle wrote, "Without friends no one would choose to live, though he had all other goods."

True friendship is a quality of giving without demand for anything in return. Friends naturally want the best for each other. But I have a feeling that it must require special qualities to be able to befriend people in the public eye, and for people in that exposed position to know who their real friends are. So many wrong motives can come into play. Kipling once wrote that a test of whether you were really mature was whether you could walk with kings and still not lose the common touch.

I was thinking of this when I read a remarkable book by a friend of mine who has indeed walked with American "kings," if one may call them that, and yet never lost that common touch, who was a close friend to some of the most famous men and women in America. He is James Newton, from Fort Myers Beach, Florida, who is 82, and has just written a most entertaining book, *Uncommon Friends* (HBJ).

To have walked just with Thomas Edison would have been a remarkable experience. To have walked with Henry Ford a revelation. To have walked with Charles Lindbergh unforgettable. Yet Jim walked with all three and more. He was like an adopted grandson to the inventor of the electric light and a vital companion to the end of his days. He was close to the car manufacturer at the height of his powers. And the aviator, at one time the most written about person in the world, was best man at Jim's wedding.

I remember being much impressed as a teenager when I was introduced by Jim to Lindbergh. Jim had met him through another towering personality, Alexis Carrel, the Nobel laureate who paved the way for modern surgery. Jim also knew Harvey Firestone well. Indeed, for a time he not only worked for him but was being groomed as the tire manufacturer's successor. One of my first memories of Jim is of him telling me how he used to fly for Firestone over busy traffic intersections; when he saw which was the busiest one, he would drop down and buy the site.

Jim has put together, using diaries, recollections, and extensive correspondence, without betraying confidences, a fascinating picture of these shapers of the twentieth century and their families. *Uncommon Friends* has a foreword by Anne Morrow Lindbergh, who describes the book as "a paean to friendship itself."

It is interesting to learn, and this is perhaps one of his strengths, that James Newton never asked to meet any of the five men. About his relationship with Edison, Firestone and Ford, Jim writes, "Perhaps my common link with all three was that I had a good pair of listening ears and a sympathetic spirit. And no axe to grind."

The extraordinary story begins when he was twenty years old and already head of development of Edison Park in Fort Myers, where the Edisons lived. Edison introduced him to Ford who in turn introduced him to Firestone. Another businessman introduced him to Carrel, which led to the friendship with the Lindberghs. Carrel and Lindbergh were featured together on the front cover of *Time* magazine in June 1938 on the day their co-authored book, *Culture of Organs*, was published.

In *Uncommon Friends* Jim takes you into the lives and homes, hopes and fears, ambitions and beliefs of these men and women as he lived, worked, and vacationed with them.

The book is crammed with telling glimpses of their lives. "Edison's deafness must often have been a burden," Jim writes, "but he never spoke of it as anything but an asset. He could read and study and work quietly no matter how much conversation surrounded him. He said his deafness had given him an excuse to sit much closer to his future wife during their courtship. He taught her the morse code when she was a teenager before they married, and they tapped out messages on the backs of each other's hands. Indeed, that was how he proposed and she accepted. He wrote in his diary, 'The word "yes" is an easy one to send by telegraph signal, and she sent it.' " Jim learned from Mrs. Edison how to talk to Edison by cupping his hand against the inventor's cheekbone, and talking through the palm so that the vibrations permitted him to hear.

For the young American who does not know what these men represented in the life of this country the book is a joyful and painless education. For the older American for whom these figures have an almost legendary quality it is a personal glimpse of the private side of their natures.

"They not only challenged my life," writes Jim, "but they changed the life of everyone living in this century. It has been said of Thomas Edison that he 'invented the twentieth century' – imagine what the world would be like without electric light or recorded sound. In most countries Henry Ford's 'automobile for the millions,' with Firestone's tires, has set the pattern for our dwellings, our communities, and our jobs. Without Alexis Carrel, how many decades would it have taken to develop modern surgery? And how much slower, without Lindbergh, would have been the shrinking of time and distance between continents or the awareness of man's need to protect our planet? These men put into our hands dynamic tools with which to shape our civilization. What have we done with them?"

Jim was certainly lucky to have such friends. But I can't help feeling that they, too, were lucky to have him, and then later his wife, Ellie. As Lindbergh wrote to Jimmy, "You are one of the most extraordinary people I have met in life. Wherever you go, you have the ability of adding to the quality of life, whether with a group or an individual. Everyone I know who has met you feels this. This is really an extraordinary gift, and I doubt you, yourself, can realize the extent of it."

I think this latter sentence is probably true. For if there is one weakness to *Uncommon Friends*, it is that we don't learn more about Jimmy. Perhaps he's saving that for another book.

July 23, 1987

Kitchen help

TWO BLOCKS from the White House, across from the World Bank and around the corner from the International Monetary Fund, in one of life's ironies, is Miriam's Kitchen. Every weekday morning 120 homeless men and women come there for breakfast, for some their one meal of the day. Until the Western Presbyterian Church opened this basement kitchen four years ago there was no other feeding program in that part of the nation's capital.

It is staffed entirely by volunteers who work from 6.30 to 8.30 each morning; and it is funded by individuals, suburban churches, and a few corporate donors. I read about Miriam's Kitchen in *Money Magazine*. I had never looked at the magazine, but neighbors asked me to pick up their mail and I opened a copy, only to see a young friend from Washington, DC, Clara Severiens, looking out at me from among pots and pans. Intrigued, I pursued the matter.

Clara, 26, has all the background and credentials for advancing on any corporate ladder. Her father was an investment banker on Wall Street. She was vice-president of her high school student body and captain of several sports, and at Princeton became president of one of the eating and social clubs around which junior and senior life revolves. She majored in politics.

But Clara also wanted to take her Christian faith seriously, and use her talents to do God's will. This helped her find what she felt was the right job – she helps non-profit organizations with their fund-raising – and also the right use of her time. She had always been interested in volunteerism. During school she had worked in a nursing home, and one summer with emotionally disturbed people. But she wanted her life to really make a difference.

Clara had what she calls a prompting to get involved with the homeless, but didn't know how and tended to dismiss the idea. One day she saw a notice at her church about Miriam's Kitchen. She thought it might be a dangerous place to work but decided to take a look. "My first reaction was exhilarating," she told me. Her volunteerism up until then had not involved her "getting down and dirty," as she puts it. But, having decided to give her talents unconditionally to God, and as organizing things was obviously one of them, she was increasingly drawn to the idea of serving regularly at the kitchen. "It was really an act of faith," she says.

That was sixteen months ago. Now she not only goes herself once a week but she has also enlisted 145 volunteers, including 73 fellow Princetonians. It is obviously important, she says, to care for the men and women who come in each day for breakfast – and she gets something important from them in return. But it is also a priority to care for the helpers. "You're building a core of volunteers," she says. "As we say about financial giving, if you've given once you're more likely to give again. It is the same with volunteering. I hope people will continue to volunteer throughout their lives."

Clara obtains her volunteers through word of mouth, through advertizing in her regional alumni club newsletter and the alumni magazine, and through turning up in her office straight from the kitchen dressed in her cooking attire of T-shirt and sweat pants. "Have you been out for a run?" she would be asked. "Actually, I've been working in a kitchen. . . ."

Her Princeton volunteers range from 18-year-old undergraduates to a former Ambassador to Senegal, Charles Bray, who, speaking about those they serve at the kitchen, told the *Princeton Alumni Weekly,* "Except for a short bend in life, any of us can be one of them, or any of them could be one of us."

Clara thinks that each of us should give not only financially but also of our time and energy. She hopes that a lot of people like herself, who have been fortunate enough to have a solid education, will be encouraged by her example to get involved and will say, "If she can do it, so can I." Many young professionals, people in graduate schools, want their lives to make a difference, she believes, but they don't always know how. "Many of us have to have the opportunity specifically presented to us. We often need that nudge that puts us over the edge," she says. "My work at the kitchen has not cut me off from anything. It has got me more involved and given me a 'can do' attitude."

The Western Presbyterian Church has asked Clara not to have her volunteers come today. There are always plenty of helpers on Thanksgiving. But tomorrow morning you can be sure they will be out again in force.

November 26, 1987

Shipwrecked on purpose

I WANT today to tell you the tale of Ranald MacDonald. No, not the clown who publicizes the Big Mac, but the Chinook Indian who spelt the Ranald name with an A instead of an O and exported himself to Japan a century before the golden arches were ever heard of.

This was more than twenty years before the Meiji Restoration when Japan sent out some of its brightest to learn from the West. This was five years before the famous entry into Tokyo Harbor of Commodore Perry and his four U.S. Navy gunboats, to begin the trade negotiations which ended Japan's self-imposed isolation. It was at a time when foreigners were equated by the Japanese with dogs, goats and barbarians. Under Japan's National Seclusion policy the country had been closed to them for 200 years, and to try to enter it was to risk execution.

Ranald MacDonald was the son of Princess Raven and of Archibald McDonald, a Hudson's Bay Company fur trading manager descended from the MacDonalds of Glencoe, Scotland. He was also a grandson of Chief Concomly of the Chinook Indians, who is credited with being the first Columbia River bar pilot. Ranald was born in what is now

Astoria and spent his boyhood at Hudson's Bay Company outposts in the US and Canada, attending Ball's School at Fort Vancouver in the first schoolhouse west of the Rockies, and finishing his formal training in Winnipeg.

I speak of him today because of the upcoming 150th anniversary of the birth of this pre-statehood Oregonian who is regarded as Japan's first teacher of English. This will be marked by a dinner seminar in Astoria organized by the Clatsop County Historical Society and the newly-formed Friends of MacDonald. One of the speakers will be Professor Torao Tomita of Rikyo University, Japan's leading authority on American Indians, who translated MacDonald's memoirs for Japanese publication in 1979. A monument to MacDonald's memory, inscribed in English and Japanese, will be dedicated.

After finishing school in 1839 Ranald worked for two years as an apprentice clerk at a bank in St. Thomas, Ontario; but the life did not agree with him, and he was spurned, it is said, by the family of a young lady he had courted. So for the next five years he roamed the world as a seaman. At the age of 24, Ranald devised a plan to circumvent the exclusion of foreigners from Japan; he would deliberately get himself shipwrecked on the Japanese coast. It is believed that his desire to do this stems from his contact with Japanese sailors shipwrecked near Cape Flattery. He became convinced that the Indians and Japanese had common ancestors. He also wanted to make friends with the Japanese people, and hoped to learn the language and be an interpreter when trade was finally established.

With the cooperation of the captain of the whaling ship *Plymouth*, Ranald was cast off in a 27-foot sailboat near the coast of Hokkaido. After three days and within sight of villagers, he deliberately capsized his boat, a stratagem he had already rehearsed several times, and was rescued by friendly Ainu fishermen. He was then taken on a journey down the coast to Nagasaki, where he was imprisoned in a temple. Treated kindly, he began to teach English to 14 scholars and learned enough Japanese to construct an English-Japanese glossary. One of his pupils, Einoske Moriyama, became Commodore Perry's interpreter, and is credited by historians with being influential in the liberalization of Japan.

After nearly a year in Japan Ranald was deported, and headed first for Australia where he joined the gold rush. He returned to British Columbia in 1853 and engaged in several businesses. In 1885 he settled near Kettle Falls, Washington, and spent his last years working on his memoir, *Japan; Story of Adventure*. He died in 1894, aged 70, and his last words, appropriately, were the Japanese farewell, "Sayonara, sayonara." His memoirs were first published thirty years later.

Ranald MacDonald is well remembered in Japan. He is featured, for instance, in the *Kodansha Encyclopedia* which I saw at the Japanese Consulate. But the two-day ceremony later this month in Astoria is the first recognition on any scale in this country of his contribution to Japanese-American relations. It will be covered by Hokkaido Television.

May 6, 1988

A ten-gallon story

THERE IS SOMETHING very American about a Stetson. And there's something very American about what has recently happened to the Stetson Company, one of America's oldest. It is a story with a happy ending – and an unhappy postscript.

A year ago the Stetson Hat Company in St. Joseph, Missouri, was in a bad way. Production was down, quality was slipping, management-labor relations were at rock bottom, and the company was reorganizing under Chapter 11.* Its

* *Federal bankruptcy provision*

leading competitor had put in a bargain basement offer to buy the company.

A local management consultant, George Sherman, was called in and was horrified by what he uncovered through an attitude survey. The employees universally distrusted both management, and the union, and each other. One employee said it was "like we are in a Communist country," another compared it with a *Stalag Luft*, another said if he had a dog he wouldn't send it to work there. "In more than thirty years of labor-management relations," said Sherman, "the Stetson situation was the worst I'd ever encountered." If the charts and graphs he developed showing labor relations health had been X-rays, he told the company management, "then without doubt the patient would be put into intensive care immediately." There was a total breakdown in communication, and extreme dissatisfaction with first line supervision, embracing such things as favoritism, verbal abuse, and a lack of concern over employee feelings.

Yet within four months, by listening to the employees, by identifying legitimate problems and doing something about them, by implementing a full-scale employee communication program, and with the backing of an enlightened management team, the bitterness dissolved and a genuine spirit of teamwork emerged.

Morale improved dramatically, with an appreciable increase in quality and productivity as well. In fact in October, the most critical month in the hat industry's year, Stetson shipped a record 70,000 hats for $2 million in sales, and did so with fewer employees than at any previous time. Just before Thanksgiving the top management people and Sherman handed out turkeys to all the employees, and the next day they received a thank you card the size of a daily newspaper signed by the employees, and including a comment by the president of the union which read, "And also thank you for treating us like human beings." Management told Sherman that they expected to be solvent and out of Chapter 11 at the beginning of 1988, and conservative forecasts put earnings over the next five years at over $10 million.

I asked Sherman how he managed to win the trust of the workers so quickly. He said it was in part thirty years experience, in part a sixth sense which workers have which tells them whether someone is sincere or is just trying to manipulate them. He also feels that he can empathize with them. His father lost his business during the depression and had to accept work as foreman of a county road gang. His own first job was washing dishes for $12 a week, then he ran a milk delivery route, worked as a timekeeper in a meatpacking plant, and was a clerk in a sporting goods store. His twelve years in journalism have also helped him to know how to communicate with everybody.

On his final day at Stetson, Sherman went through the plant to say goodbye. "It was heart-warming," he says, "to have so many thank me for helping to make their lives and their work more rewarding."

Ironically, Stetson's successful turnaround was its undoing. The improved quality and production was beginning to cut into the sales of the main competitor. The competitor upped his offer for the company substantially and, taking advantage of a family squabble, succeeded in buying it out. The new management has fired the team that turned the company around, so Stetson's future in St. Joseph is now a question mark.

Sherman believes that despite this "sad aftermath," the Stetson example may serve as an incentive for other good-intentioned managements experiencing labor problems to try to do something constructive. In his view the inroads of foreign competition are more effectively dealt with in this way, with improved quality and productivity, than with trade barriers or a trade war.

"The message to America," Sherman told me, "is that American workers want to work and are willing to work, and can out-perform any workers in the world if only management will listen to them and demonstrate concern for their worth and dignity as human beings."

April 14, 1988

A proper Bostonian

SALLY was in her seventies when I first got to know her. I travelled with her in Europe, Asia and America. She was one of a number of remarkable older American women I have met over the years who have amazed me by their stamina, their indomitable spirit, their readiness to accept new challenges. Most of them do not appear in reference books or get remembered in a week like this when we honor women in history. But they made significant contributions all the same. Sally certainly did.

Sarah Lawrence Slattery, to give her her proper name, and one should give her proper name, for she was a Bostonian of the Bostonians, the daughter of a bishop, the sister of two bishops, and the widow of a bishop; and she lived on Beacon Street. I recall her saying once, "I used to pray to God every night to make me better, but I didn't see how he could." She was an Episcopalian of the type once described as "starched and ironed without being washed." "I was so upright," she once joked, "I used to fall over backwards."

She could joke in this way because she had a remarkable change of lifestyle and purpose when she met Moral Re-Armament, or the Oxford Group as it was then called. In her autobiography, *I Choose* (University Press), she refers to her first foray with a team of six people in 1934. It was to Portland and other West Coast cities and one of her group, Charles Malik from Lebanon, was later to become a president of the General Assembly of the United Nations. When I travelled with her for six months in India in 1952–3, she was coping with the rigors of the trip, the heat, the unfamiliar diet, the living out of a suitcase, just as well as some of us who were 50 years younger. And her commitment and change were a challenge to all she met. Her nephew, Samuel A. Lawrence, described his aunt as "a lady born to privilege and trained in the conservative traditions of New England who embraced a commitment in later life to an all-out action program of world change."

She has a certain claim to recognition in Women in History week, for she was the founder of the Junior League of Boston in 1905.

Sally had developed early on a strong social conscience. Attending the Simmons College School for Social Work in Boston she was given the chance to hear such figures as Booker T. Washington, Dr. W. E. B. DuBois, and Jane Addams. Learning of the initiative of three ladies in New York who had formed themselves into a Junior League, it seemed to her to be just what was needed in Boston. She described them as "girls of privilege who took up seriously the idea of making friends and breaking down barriers between people of all classes and conditions." She went on to help organize the first national meeting, and the Boston Junior League helped spread the idea across the country. That work of breaking down barriers was to become a life task and to find its world expression in Moral Re-Armament.

Today the Junior League continues the dedication to volunteerism pioneered by those women earlier in the century in New York and Boston. There are 258 Junior Leagues with a membership of over 160,000 in the US, Canada, Mexico, and Britain.

In Portland more than 1200 women participate in the League's work and training, in areas of social service, family advocacy, historic preservation and public policy. The League is totally self-supporting, returning 70% of its revenue to the community, more than $1¼ million. "The Portland community and the options available to women have changed greatly since our beginnings in 1910," says Junior League President Lynette Houghton. "What has not changed is our commitment to what women can achieve as volunteers in service to their community."

Sally would have approved. She was serving until she died, in her nineties.

March 6, 1986

Driving a hard bargain

LABOR DAYS just come and go. For most people they seem to signal only the end of the American summer, just as Memorial Days do the beginning. Neither day exists in England where I grew up, our nearest equivalent being May Day on May 1 and Armistice Day on November 11; and we take our summer when we find it!

Although the celebration of Labor Day was first inaugurated in New York by the Knights of Labor in 1882, it was, in fact, Oregon which exactly 100 years ago was the first state to legislate for its observance as a legal holiday. At that time it was the first Saturday in June. In 1893 it was changed to the present first Monday in September.

Labor Days nowadays mark for most people a laborless three-day holiday, not an honoring of working people. But a friend who was in our home recently has reason to remember Labor Day as a turning point in his life which was to affect the well-being of thousands of workers.

On a Labor Day weekend nearly thirty years ago John Moore and his wife attended a Moral Re-Armament industrial conference. He was then a young employee in the Scovill Manufacturing Company. It was an international conference where those from management and labor were meeting on the basis of finding "not who's right but what's right," and where the emphasis was not on faulting others but on discovering where you could start to put things right yourself.

John Moore felt that this approach could be beneficial at Scovill and persuaded his bosses to send a joint management-labor group to the sessions. He accompanied them. "It had a profound effect on the thinking of all of us," John told me. Each began to show an interest in what the other side was doing, and mutual trust developed.

It was not always easy, particularly for the union officials, who were accused by some colleagues of being soft. But as they worked together, they were able to move from a strongly adversarial position to one, if not of complete cooperation, where they were achieving a common goal of making the company a good place to work, free from labor strife, where people were convinced they were trying to do the right thing. The plant where John worked, in Waterbury, Connecticut, was the largest in the Scovill operation, employing some 5000, and in a way John was setting a pilot relationship there for the company. The plant became strike free. In 1960 he was appointed chief negotiator for the whole company. Six years later he became Director of Corporate Employee Relations, and in 1968, Vice-President. And what happened at Waterbury became the norm throughout the company.

At its peak Scovill was doing nearly a billion dollars of business a year, at 52 plants around the world with 20,000 employees. John had to deal with ten international unions and 30 locals including names familiar to all like the IAM, the IUE, the IBEW, the UAW and the Teamsters. "They recognized," he says, "that we drove a hard bargain but a fair one, and that we were not out to destroy their organizations or their elected officials." To date, he says, out of 600 million man-hours worked, only 300 thousand have been lost due to labor disputes.

John says that what was achieved was, of course, not unique. Nor would he like to claim credit for it. He was building, he says, on good work done by his predecessors and by colleagues who welcomed this approach. But he points to two basic changes that came into his life at that Labor Day weekend which played a part.

One was the willingness to listen for God's guidance. During his career, guidance had told him again and again that his place was in employee relations whenever he was tempted to go into line management and avoid a lot of hassle. Guidance had also shown him practical steps to take in difficult negotiations.

For instance, in the first major negotiations he was involved in after returning from the conference, when things were hot and heavy, as he puts it, he felt sure that it would be useful if God would speak to him and show him "some bright way out." But as he listened, the only thought he got was, "Do not return evil for evil." He realized it meant that in facing all the attacks on the company and its motives, he should resist the temptation to strike back, to indulge in mudslinging. He followed the thought, he said, despite his nature which is very competitive – as befits one who anchored the Yale University swim team when it established a world relay record.

The other change was to accept absolute moral standards of honesty, purity, unselfishness and love as measuring rods for his life. He realized that there were wrong things in his life that should be put right. So he decided to straighten up affairs from college, like paying his poker debts. "The absolutes are essential," he believes. "They have made a difference all through my life. They are important for people in business and labor. You need above all the ability to read people, and you read people a whole lot better if you have been able to clean up in your own life what's been askew. In our work we had to help people become the people they were meant to be. You can preach all you like, but what works is example."

John Moore is still a consultant to the Scovill Corporation, and is also using his skills in bringing people together to improve relations with China and with Japan where he goes from time to time. In fact, he is one of the sponsors of an annual, and beneficial, encounter in Switzerland between senior figures in Japanese and Western industries.

And it all, as he points out, goes back to Labor Day. So, who knows, perhaps your weekend too will have some surprising repercussions.

September 3, 1987

7 Flying the flag

"This is Michael. He's originally from Britain." I am often introduced in this sort of way. To tell you the truth, I don't feel comfortable with the "originally." As far as I am concerned I am still from Britain.

As a family we try and return to England regularly and we subscribe to English publications to keep us up to date. From time to time, too, I comment on things British.

It is a changing Britain. A little English boy was asked what he would like to be when he grew up – a doctor, a fireman, a policeman, a prime minister? "Oh, no," he interrupted, "that's a woman's job."

All but doomed

PAUL THEROUX in his book, *The Kingdom by the Sea*, refers at one point to the "doomed Llanwern steelworks." As an Englishman I found his book excessively gloomy, peopled by rather sad characters, and I would like to have introduced him to another side of British life. So I was much heartened to read this week that, far from being doomed, Llanwern is now attracting world attention for the way it has helped turn around the fortunes of the British steel industry.

Theroux is right. It *was* doomed. It was all but written off. The British Steel Corporation was losing over ten thousand pounds for each of its 166,400 employees, and Llanwern had the worst reputation of all its plants – in labor relations, productivity, low quality, high price and failure to meet delivery dates. It had never, even in the good years of the steel industry, been profitable. It was the 13th loss-making British steel plant due for closure.

Then, suddenly, without a penny of new investment, Llanwern began to turn around. An article in the *South Wales Argus* in 1983, when the steelworks' future was still in jeopardy, said, "You cannot lay your hands on the reason and pull it out of a hat like a magician to place before the British Steel Corporation Board or the government. But you can feel it. Put simply, it's the overwhelming determination of the ordinary workers at the plant to make sure Llanwern survives. It has already worked what has become known as "the Llanwern miracle" – turning what was not so long ago a stumbling giant into a sleek greyhound which has outpaced many of its rivals in the efficiency race. The figures speak for themselves. In the last few weeks the plant has been shattering its own output records and achieving productivity figures that can equal or better its top European rivals."

The Chairman of British Steel not only reprieved the plant but decided to make it the standard for the restructuring of the whole corporation. To become competitive British Steel's workforce had to be cut by three quarters, but the Llanwern experience contributed to the manner and spirit in which the restructuring was carried out, so that cooperation rather than confrontation became the norm. When Sir Charles Villiers, former head of the British Steel Corporation, was in Portland, he told us of the efforts the company was making to help provide employment for those who lost their jobs. Indeed, BSC Industry, which was set up to do this job under his chairmanship, has given support to 2,700 new businesses around the nation which have generated some 70,000 jobs.

Now British Steel, as *The Economist* reports, "is arguably the most successful steel company in Europe." In 1985 British Steel made its first profits in ten years, and analysts predict that this year's profits will be £400 million.

What happened at Llanwern seems to be the product of all sides, management, labor and government, moving beyond recrimination. "We in management had to change our attitudes and working practices," admits Llanwern Plant Director Bill Harrison, while worker director David Williams says the trade unions at Llanwern were prepared to accept their share of the blame for what had gone wrong in the past. It was the product, too, of individuals who in their thinking and planning went way beyond their usual responsibilities. "People are putting in a tremendous personal commitment," commented a section manager. Jim Foley, South Wales Regional Secretary of the main steelworkers' union, summed it up, "Llanwern was saved by a team effort."

A trade union branch secretary, for instance, put aside his hatred of the Establishment and forged links with the Conservative government. He met with industrialists, whom he found to be as concerned as he that industry should work for the benefit of all. Customers came in to meet with the steelmen. "We will tell you why we no longer buy your steel," said one of them, "and you can tell us why we should." Management made a full disclosure of information so that trust was established. "There is an open door policy to us," said a union leader. And as employees began to feel responsible and included in decisions, production improved from 10 man hours per ton of steel to 3.27. With new confidence government has been able to invest seven billion pounds in the industry as a whole over the past decade.

The London *Times* wrote, "Management-union relationships have never been better, craft and process worker demarcation lines have dissolved and such a commitment and determination to succeed is evident everywhere. The vigor and vitality which is almost tangible seems paradoxical at a time when the steel industry is experiencing its deepest crisis since the Thirties."

I hope someone can pass on this news to Paul Theroux.

February 18, 1988

When the barriers rise

THE THREAT of a tidal wave on the Oregon coast reminded me of flood scares in London. When we last lived there our home was in Westminster, not far from the Thames river, which in London also rises and falls with the tide. One day notices went up on lampposts around alerting us to the possibility of flooding and directing what we should do if the river overflowed its banks. There was even the testing of air raid alarm type sirens. It wasn't a theoretical threat.

The Greater London Council, as it was then called, reckoned that it was only a matter of time before London would be flooded, the greatest natural disaster ever to hit Britain.

If this happened, more than a million people who live in London's low-lying areas would be at risk, as well as a quarter of a million homes, factories and offices. Transport would come to a standstill in Central London, with many main line train stations out of action, and the Underground (subway) system could be paralyzed for six months. Many hospitals, major sewage works, fire and ambulance stations could be under water. Communications would be disrupted and water supplies contaminated. The Houses of Parliament, most government offices, and New Scotland Yard could be under three feet of water for a day. The direct cost of a major flood in London is put at around £4 billion. Some people feel the city would never recover.

London was severely flooded in 1236 and in 1663, and in recent years the level of the Thames has come close to flooding. In 1965 water lapped within six inches of overtopping the river walls in Central London. In 1976 an eight and a half foot surge tide coincided, fortunately, with low tide. In January 1978, the time we lived through, record 82 mph northerly winds brought the Thames to within two feet of the top of London's flood defenses.

Geologists say that Britain is slowly tilting, causing London and the South-East to dip downwards at the rate of one foot every hundred years. At the same time high tides are getting higher, with the result that today's tides are more than two feet higher at London Bridge than they were 100 years ago. If, on top of that, bad weather conditions in the North Atlantic and the North Sea were to create a storm surge tide, then London, experts believe, would suffer a catastrophe on the scale of the Great Fire. Statistically, the chance of overtopping the river's flood defenses is about once in 50 years, but with rising tides the danger increases every year.

Now for the good news!

The inevitability of a disastrous flood has concentrated the bureaucratic mind wonderfully and spurred the ingenuity of the British engineer. To protect London the civic authorities have built the largest moveable flood barrier in the world at Woolwich and raised the river banks down stream to Barking and Dartford Creeks. The Barrier took eight years to build, went into operation two years ahead of schedule and cost over 500 million pounds. It was officially opened in 1984 and is being publicized to tourists as "the eighth wonder of the world."

The Barrier spans 570 yards across the Thames and

consists of 10 separate moveable steel gates, each pivoting and supported between concrete piers, which house the hydraulic machinery that operates them. Half a million tons of concrete went into the construction, enough to build nine miles of six-lane freeway.

When they are raised, each of the four main gates stands 52 feet high; they are as wide as the opening of Tower Bridge and weigh more than a naval destroyer. When not in use, the gates lie recessed in the river bed, the four largest being each the size of half a football field. This allows shipping to navigate the Thames normally. The gates are built with two inch steel to withstand the blow of a wayward ship. They are manned all the year round and can be closed in half an hour. The operating and maintenance cost of the Barrier is about three million pounds a year.

Already the Barrier is proving a popular tourist attraction. Alongside the construction is a visitor center with an audio-visual presentation and an exhibition about the need for the Barrier and how it operates. It has a buffet service, a coffee shop, a licensed bar and a souvenir shop. Boats run regularly to it from Greenwich and Westminster Piers and there are good rail, road and bus connections.

An American friend, Elsie Bailey, who was recently in London, tells me that she went by boat from Greenwich and was much impressed. The Barrier, she said, resembled a lot of sunken ships with their bows sticking up out of the water. Her guide had told her that the Barrier had been raised once, during a dangerous tide over the last Christmas holidays, and "had already paid for itself with that closing."

London can now confidently expect a welcome flood — of visitors.

August 7, 1986

Fire engine for Africa

THE LINKING of cities and states with their counterparts in other countries – twinning as it is termed in Europe – has been going on for many years, contributing to international understanding.

The US equivalent, the Sister City movement, was inaugurated by President Eisenhower in 1956 as the "People-to-People program," with the aim of establishing friendship and understanding between the people of the United States and the peoples of other nations through direct contact. A national organization, Sister Cities International, oversees the administration of the 1200 current programs. There are 23 Oregon Sister Cities, with others pending. Portland has already been approached by more than a dozen suitor cities around the world, and, as there are some 150 or so possible countries, the city has rightly felt it necessary to draw up criteria for establishing new links. These criteria address such matters as local support, common interest, and an adequate financial base, as the city will provide some services to the sister city but no dowry.

One of the world's most innovative twinning arrangements, indeed one that is broad, unique, and involves two whole nations, came to my attention recently. A Welsh friend of mine, Paul Williams, I learned, was just back from Lesotho. I knew his connections with India. What in the world was he doing in Southern Africa, I asked.

Five years ago Paul convened in Bangor, a "Dialogue on Wales' role." The invitation asked, "In the light of our unique position and experience, what can be Wales' contribution towards solving the dilemmas facing us in the UK, in Europe and the world? In which areas can Wales make its best contribution?"

The dialogue drew together people from different parties, churches, and areas of the country. One who attended was Dr. Carl Clowes, a medical health adviser and planner and a campaigner for the Welsh language. While some were saying that Wales could do nothing without its own government or power, Carl said, "Yes, there are things we can do." And he put forward the idea of Wales finding a small developing country of its own size that it could get to understand, relate to, and "twin" with.

Reviewing the results of the dialogue Paul and his friends felt this was the idea to undergird. As a result, in August 1983 during the National Eisteddfod, the famous gathering of choirs in Wales, a Steering Committee was set up which had Dr. Clowes as Chairman, Paul as Secretary, and included leaders of the principal political parties.

The idea which they pursued was to build a relationship between two national communities which, economically, were in different "halves" of the world. Lesotho was chosen because of its size and similarities with Wales – mountainous terrain, hill farming, bilingualism, a growing accent on tourism and on the use of precious water resources, a mining tradition, an enthusiasm for education and for choral singing.

So two years ago on March 12, Lesotho National Day, the link, known in Welsh as *Dolen Cymru*, was launched at a ceremony in Cardiff. It was attended by the then Lesotho High Commissioner, O. T. Sefako, who said that it represented "a new pattern in international relations."

Since then the idea has flowered. Already 22 Welsh schools have links with their counterparts. One Wrexham school, for instance, has a Lesotho week and regular Lesotho assemblies. Welsh women's organizations have supplied 4500 blankets to Lesotho's children. Children's wards are linking up with children's wards, clubs with clubs, districts with districts. The Lesotho Police have accepted the offer, made by a Welsh county fire service, of a fully-equipped fire engine. The Anglican and Methodist parishes of Bangor have ties with the parishes in Maseru, the capital. Welsh trade unions have written to the Lesotho unions. As part of the UN Year of the Shelter, the Welsh are getting involved, too, in low cost housing in Lesotho.

Other possibilities being explored are bonds between farming associations, universities, and water authorities. *Dolen Cymru* is now publishing a Welsh and English language newsletter which describes the burgeoning contacts and has set up a permanent center in Wrexham. Lesotho exhibits were a feature of the National Welsh Eisteddfod and the Royal Welsh show, and it is proposed that the Maseru Teachers Choir take part in next year's Llangollen International Eisteddfod. A record and cassette with contributions from choirs in both countries has been released.

Paul is just back, as I mentioned, from a trip to Lesotho along with Dr. Clowes. There they met with the committee approved by the Lesotho Council of Ministers to handle arrangements at that end. They were interviewed on the radio and in the press, visited schools, hospitals, and colleges, spoke at many occasions, and had 65 meetings in two weeks. They conveyed a message from the Secretary of State for Wales in which he expressed the hope that the visit would serve to strengthen and enlarge contacts between Wales and Lesotho "which can only be of benefit to both peoples."

"We have always emphasized", Paul wrote me this week, "that this is a link between people, organizations and communities at the 'grass roots' level not 'at the top.' It is not government originated or controlled, though we are grateful for the 'blessing' of the authorities on both sides and recognize that this is essential if the 'twinning' is to work. We are equally clear that we in Wales are not another aid organization and that the link is more about understanding, friendship, and interchange than about giving aid. If material assistance is forthcoming, it will have been generated from real understanding and genuine perception of need – as one friend would want to help another."

March 12, 1987

Left for dead

THIS SUMMER I met Horacio, a young Argentinian conscript who fought in the Falklands-Malvinas war. His had been an extraordinary brush with fate, being left for dead on the battlefield, wrapped in a blanket on a pile of corpses. A British sergeant, in tears, came by checking names and putting bodies in bags. As Horacio was being examined his eyes blinked – and the sergeant was able to take him to a medical crew who saved his life. When I met him he was setting off with some trepidation on a first visit to England.

In September I noticed in our Cable TV guide the announcement of a program, "The Falklands War – the Untold Story." I switched on, and there, along with soldiers, politicians and diplomats from both sides, was Horacio telling his story. The two-hour program, made by Yorkshire Television, was a sensitive portrayal of the war, at times gruesome, causing you to reflect on the waste of young lives and on how little the art of peacemaking has caught up with the art of making war.

Here were two of America's closest allies fighting each other over a desolate piece of real estate in the South Atlantic. It was a war in which a thousand died and a thousand were wounded, with a victory for Britain which meant that Thatcher stayed in office and Galtieri in Argentina was removed, and which in a curious way led to Argentina's democracy today. Yet it made you realize that better ways must be found of resolving potential conflicts before they escalate to war. "The whole affair," as one commando major said, "was one of tragedy. It was savage, gutter fighting."

Images and impressions remain, first of all, of courage. The charismatic colonel who died leading an attack on a particularly difficult emplacement; and the young marine who went back to almost certain death below decks to rescue a fellow soldier, failed to get him out, was himself rescued, tried to commit suicide because he had failed, and then had the "most incredible feeling," as he described it, when the padre was able to take him to the man he thought was dead.

To go back had been, he said, "the biggest deciding point in my life."

Images of stupidity. The British officer who refused to accept the advice to get his men off an exposed ship, only to see them killed in an explosion; and the Argentine military *junta* who couldn't agree on the terms of a settlement being negotiated by the United States. And the day by day momentum southwards of an armada that never thought it was actually going to have to fight.

Images of humanity. The British airman paying tribute to a brave Argentine pilot who kept on coming when common sense would have said that he should take the chance to save his life. The wounded being treated as wounded regardless of nationality. Horacio asking, as he returned to an Argentina so remote in spirit from what he had lived through, "How many fathers did I kill? What are we supposed to do now?" And the English widow, whose husband's pipe, wristwatch, St. Christopher, and wedding ring were returned to her in a plastic pouch, admitting to a surge of bitterness when she saw those who came home safely, and saying, "No one will ever know what price we paid. But perhaps it was worth it for Britain's sake."

Images of insensitivity. The headline "Gotcha" in an English tabloid when the *Admiral Belgrano* was sunk, contrasted with the selfless example of Lord Carrington, minister responsible when the Falklands were occupied. "The honorable thing is to resign," he said, and he did. The euphoria of victory, with bunting, bands, and parades, contrasted with participants who would rather have gone quietly home as they saw a nation that was enjoying its holiday on the beaches as usual, reveling in victory for perhaps the wrong reasons, and having no idea what hell they had all been through.

I had a postscript recently, a letter about Horacio's visit to London. He had asked to meet the British commander of a parachute regiment against whom he had fought. The commander didn't want to, but finally agreed. The atmosphere was charged with emotion as they met. They embraced. The British commander broke into tears. A bridge was built.

Perhaps five years after the war, servicemen will lead the way to resolving outstanding differences that still persist between two countries who are meant to be friends.

September 10, 1987

Prince Charles

THE LAST EMPEROR is a superb film which deserves all its Oscars. Beautifully shot in China, it is a tragic story of a young ruler thrown out into a world from which he had by upbringing been isolated, and for whose pressures he was unprepared. His subsequent deterioration of character made him easy meat for a rapacious regime.

Britain's Queen Elizabeth is no longer an Empress, and Britain's royal family, like other royal families today, is much less the product of an unreal world. In fact our present Queen, through her years of weekly meetings with her prime ministers and her close knowledge of Commonwealth leaders, must be the best informed head of state in the world. Her personal qualities, and the example set by most of her family, have had a beneficial and stabilizing effect on British life.

The heir to the throne, Prince Charles, was educated at schools in England and Australia, attended Cambridge University, and made his way as a naval officer. He tries within limits to lead a normal life and, in fact, very nearly died recently when a Swiss avalanche claimed the life of one of his best friends while they were skiing. Prince Charles is increasingly listened to, and as a result gets attacked and is vulnerable because he cannot answer back. He has had in silence to endure constant insinuations about his family life. The latest criticism of him has come from the former

Conservative Party chairman, Norman Tebbit, who suggested on BBC television that the Prince felt extra sympathy towards unemployed people because he also has no job – until he inherits the throne.

Prince Charles is constantly depicted in this way as being frustrated because as heir to the throne his duties are circumscribed and he cannot be fulfilled. It may be true, as the *Daily Express* claimed after Tebbit's attack, that his workload is thin and that he has yet to find a function in which he can more fully exercise his talents. I have no way of knowing. But, as the paper also rightly points out, Prince Charles is no idle pleasure seeker like some of his royal predecessors, and he has a knack of coming up with ideas that politicians have not thought of.

I am of the view that the analysis of the Heir Apparent as unfulfilled is a view of those who measure all life in materialist terms of position and self-growth, and not by the Christian yardstick of what does it do for others.

It is possible, as a recent piece in the *New York Times* suggested, that the Prince is obsessed with what to do with the rest of his life. He admits, "I've had to fight every inch of my life to escape royal protocol. I am determined not to be confined to cutting ribbons." But he is slowly becoming what one of his friends calls a "needle in the conscience" of Britain on important social issues.

He has taken initiative or spoken out on a wide variety of issues, from the problems of inner cities and of youth employment, to modern architectural shortcomings and the threat of acid rain from factories and pollution from cars.

I regard the latest attack as an indication that possibly that "needle of conscience" is beginning to make itself felt where it ought to be, at the heart of Britain's Establishment. Prince Charles has a fine line to tread. He is not allowed to become embroiled in party political matters and will have to choose carefully what controversial issues he should raise.

But it is what he is as a man, rather than what he does or even what he says, that will both satisfy him and inspire the nation. He will not one day be "King Emperor" as his grandfather was, but he will be "Defender of the Faith". So it is appropriate that he sees his job as "more than anything else a way of life."

April 29, 1988

Sharp practice

HOW MANY creative ideas are lost to the world because our minds are cluttered with unhelpful input or clouded with preoccupations which could be got rid of? I thought about this when I considered the story of a friend in Liverpool.

Fifteen years ago Jim Sharp was a partner in a small commercial artists' firm doing distinctive work of high quality. But his marriage of ten years was coming apart, and he was, as his wife Rita says, "a martyr to the booze." Today Jim hasn't touched a drop for some ten years, employs 70 people in a city desperately needing jobs, and has developed a new way of getting high definition in printing which has caught the attention of the printing industry around the world.

He believes that God, who told him to stop drinking, also gave him the idea for this new printing process.

The story began in 1973 when Rita accepted an invitation to attend a theatrical production about Moral Re-Armament in London. She didn't expect her husband to come with her as there would be no drink at the event. She had become accustomed to making her own life, having fostered about 40 children over the years. But he rather aggressively told her he could do without the drink and would come. "I wore a purple suit and long hair," he says. "I was trying to establish my identity, put my stamp on the world."

A basic principle of Moral Re-Armament, to which the Sharps were introduced in London and in subsequent meetings in Liverpool, was the idea that if an individual took time in quiet to listen to God, he or she might get thoughts that would be helpful to their lives and to the world. After one quiet time Jim had the distinct thought to give up drinking. "I used to be a boozer," he says. "I'd come home sloshed, but I said it was all part of my work, keeping the customers happy." Rita was skeptical at first. "I hadn't much faith, I expected him to lapse," she recalls. But Jim persisted. It was obvious, for one thing, that he was taking a new interest in his family as a result. He began to spend more time at home in the evenings.

"Rita noticed a slight change," says Jim. "Slight!" exclaims Rita. "It was like Jekyll and Hyde. I'm deeply grateful. Jim's change saved our marriage. I still don't find faith in God easy, but he's the first person I call on when I'm in trouble."

As a commercial artist Jim had often felt frustrated by the poor quality of reproduction when his designs appeared in newspapers. One night Jim got the inspiration for a process which could create a crisper image. "In his drinking days he would have been flat out," says Rita. He talked it over with her through the night – and the next morning went straight to the patent office. "It was a gift from God," he says.

The new process, Schafline, brought fresh business; but there were still problems, work pressures, and personality conflicts. Again, however, he felt God was giving him clear direction, this time to leave the firm. "I felt a different man once I'd done it, but I didn't know where to go next," he says. For six months before the decision, Rita says, he was aggressive and horrible. Once he had made it he went back to being his normal, cheerful self.

He offered to sell his half of the company to his partner but the offer was refused, so Jim started his own business. A little later his former partner offered to sell to him, and Jim decided to buy him out. Without Jim the company had been going down hill fast, and he felt he shouldn't let the staff down. It took him days on the phone to recover clients, but since then the company has not looked back. From 25 employees at that point it has grown to 70, work has increased 30 to 40% each year, advertizements processed by Schafline increasingly appear in Britain's national press, and franchises have been negotiated with companies in Canada and the United States.

As well as giving up drink, he says, he has also learned to accept absolute honesty as a principle for operating his business, refusing to give unofficial commissions or look for opportunities to fiddle. "It means," he says, "that you get a much clearer view ahead of how to plan for yourself and your company; you can justify your prices with vigor, and look your customer straight in the eye."

Working also on the basis of "what's right not who's right" has reduced personality clashes at the company. "Then you don't have a winner or a loser," he says, "and you get all the brains working together on the problem." There are regular meetings of the production staff, and they know they can always talk with him. A good relationship has also been established with the trade union, the National Graphical Association. At the end of the year a chunk of profits goes into staff bonuses amounting to almost eight percent of their annual income. "If someone is doing substandard work," Jim says, "fellow workers keep him up to the mark, not management, as their part of the bargain." He believes in training others to do the job better than himself. So though he occasionally puts in an 18-hour day – over half of Schafline's work has to be completed within 24 hours – he still is able to take plenty of time with his family.

The company name is well known and the work pours in, and to Rita's continual surprise not one of Jim's clients has he met in a pub. Jim's American associate, John Schaedler, had earlier failed to negotiate an agreement with the company before Jim owned it, and had gone ahead and developed a similar process. Three years ago Jim visited him in New York. Schaedler's company magazine, *Pinwheel Pink Pages*, wrote, "Expecting to be punched in the nose, Schaedler found Sharp, on the contrary, to be quite agreeable, conciliatory, and in fact rather a delightful fellow. The meeting ended with a handshake, and both agreed to help each other expand their respective businesses."

August 20, 1987

God's politician

THERE ARE not too many examples in history of nations having moved beyond self-interest, and certainly not enough examples of individuals in public life having done so. At the national level one thinks immediately of the Marshall Plan and America's generous treatment of her former enemies at the end of World War II. At the individual level one thinks of courageous resignations by people who disagreed with policy.

One of the most remarkable in all history, a combination of both, was brought to my attention this week with the publication of a new book, *God's Politician* (Helmers and Howard). It is subtitled "William Wilberforce's struggle to abolish the Slave Trade and reform the morals of a nation."

William Lecky, in his work, *History of European Morals*, describes Britain's crusades against slavery as probably "among the three or four perfectly virtuous pages comprised in the history of nations." And Historian G. M. Trevelyan calls Abolition "one of the turning events in the history of the world." *God's Politician* is the enthralling story of what it took in vision, dedication, and imagination to swing a whole country behind this new, and right, direction.

It has become fashionable in some quarters to suggest that Britain ended the slave trade because it was no longer a money-maker. But author Garth Lean points out, very much to the contrary, that the slave trade was ended when it was at its most profitable. This makes the story all the more remarkable.

I hope some movie maker picks up the rights to this book, because it has all the elements of a gripping saga. It could even be a miniseries. There is bribery and corruption, with political skullduggery of every kind, tragedy and disappointment, religion and politics, and, of course, racial prejudice. There is nobility and sacrifice, and it spans a tumultuous 50-year period of history that was characterized by cruelty and decadence. The cast of characters includes John Wesley, who with his dying breath urged Wilberforce to persevere in the struggle; and it stars William Wilberforce, the frail, sickly, shrimp of a man who in his early twenties gave up the chance to be Prime Minister, by adopting this unpopular and giant-sized cause, and who on his deathbed 46 years later was given the news that within the year all 800,000 slaves in British territories were to be set free.

As a young man Wilberforce wrote in the journal that he kept, "God Almighty has set before me two great objects – the suppression of the slave trade and the reformation of manners," by which today we would mean the whole moral and spiritual state of the country. Wilberforce felt that if the slave trade and its ramifications were destroyed, it would be a key factor in bringing a new spirit into the nation. He also felt there must be a change in people before institutions would change.

God's Politician describes the battle to achieve both objectives, and Wilberforce's commitment to what in a bestseller of his day which he authored, he called "real Christianity." To give some idea of the breadth of what was achieved I would simply note that while maintaining the pressure on the slave trade, Wilberforce and his colleagues promoted education for the masses, championed prison reform, attacked child labor and savage game laws, opposed flogging in the army, supported and introduced every bill in Parliament to change factory conditions, fought for Catholic emancipation, and even intervened on behalf of victims in other countries including the native Americans. They also founded the Church Missionary Society and the British and

Foreign Bible Society. In the first year of their campaign they brought out two million books, and by its 50th anniversary their religious tract society had published 5000 different titles and 500 million copies. The work of the "Clapham saints," as they were called, laid the groundwork for many of the important reforms and democratic developments that followed.

It is an incredible story, and wonderfully told by author Garth Lean. He has written the book, he says, to tackle one of the cruelest illusions of our day, the idea that the individual is helpless to do anything to alter events around him. He believes the world is waiting to see which countries will today produce the bands of committed people who will tackle the insuperable problems of the coming age, as Wilberforce and his friends tackled the deadlocked situations of their times.

In a foreword Chuck Colson writes, "Here was a Christian who put his faith into action in the political arena and persevered for years to outlaw one of the most inhumane and profitable practices in the world of his day. His battle cost not only the national self-interest but also his own. This little man with the piercing blue eyes and upturned nose stands as a giant in the modern history of the faith. He was truly God's politician."

March 3, 1988

8   Around the globe

An English doctor stayed with us in Portland. He was impressed with the medical facilities here, as he had been also with an exhibition of modern medical equipment in Sweden. He had seen there at least five different forms of brain scanners, each costing between 500 and 700 thousand dollars.

A few weeks after being in Sweden, he flew to India and found himself one day in a village, sitting crosslegged in front of a temple as the villagers gave thanks for the visit of an old man. This man who was over seventy had been a disciple of Mahatma Gandhi. As a young man he had asked the Mahatma what he should do with his life. Gandhi replied that he should use it to teach simple hygiene to the villagers of Maharashtra.

For many years he had done just that, earning no salary but just travelling from village to village, teaching them how to build toilets, how to use the manure they produced, and how to clean up the water supply. In return, all he asked for was somewhere to lie down and some food during his stay in the village. To build toilets he required only the tools which the villagers had, and a few readily available items which cost a few *paisa*, a few cents, each.

"The simple truth," my doctor friend told me, "is that this old man will have saved more lives than the sophisticated Western technology."

Collision or collusion

THE SUMMIT meeting brings to mind some words of Rudyard Kipling:

> When pack meets with pack in the jungle,
> And neither will go from the trail,
> Lie down till the leaders have spoken,
> It may be fair words shall prevail.

The leaders have spoken, fair words have prevailed, and somehow for most of us the jungle seems that little bit safer this week. It is in part an illusion, of course. Both packs still have the same capacity for ferocity and could tear each other apart. The democratic pack leader is probably no wiser than he was yesterday. The communist pack leader has done nothing that absolves us from looking at his country's appalling record rather than his appealing rhetoric.

But the ordinary animals of the forest have seen the glimpse of a hope, that we could turn away from the madness of policies which may have provisionally kept the peace but have inevitably increased the fear. Reducing for the first time in history our nuclear weaponry, it is just possible we could be entering what strategist Edward Luttwak has termed the "postnuclear age."

A veteran British Ambassador, Adam Watson, speaking in Portland last week, described the US and the USSR as a pair of bookends for the international system, keeping it in order. Europeans, he said, fear a collision between the two or collusion, but they also want the lessening of tension the INF* treaty could produce.

The treaty in itself will solve little and may well create more problems, in particular for European defense planners. Yet it has incorporated more verification measures, including onsite inspection in the USSR, than many would have deemed possible. And as Max Kampelman, the Chief US Negotiator says, "We can't blow them away, we can't wish them away

* *Intermediate Nuclear Forces*

We have to find a formula by which we can live with them in peace and dignity."

The cold war in varying temperatures has ruled attitudes for the entire life of most inhabitants on today's earth. We will live with its fallout for a long time. Communism and freedom are incompatible. They may have to coexist but we must not blur the distinction. Yet. without being naive, we need to recognize that there is another, perhaps more fundamental, struggle in the world where each of us can have immediate input.

Dividing the world into two blocs is a convenient simplification, but it may obscure the fact that there is a tremendous force of selfish materialism at work in both, that spirit which puts things before people, which makes us one in our need of change. Cardinal Koenig, former Archbishop of Vienna, goes as far as to say that he sees little difference between the organized materialism of the communist world and the disorganized materialism of the non-communist world.

"People in the East as well as the West," he says, "need to look deep inside themselves and to discover the conscience that the Creator implanted there, the source of spirit and truth. Honest, frank dialogue growing from Christian roots can overturn the walls that have seemed insurmountable."

Through the INF treaty our leaders have breached the nuclear wall. If we take the Cardinal's words seriously, we may see other walls in the jungle crumble as well.

December 11, 1987

Give us bad news

THE CRACK TROOPS from the Commando battalions of the Zimbabwe National Army marched smartly past as their President, Robert Mugabe, took the salute. The occasion: the dedication of the new war memorial at their Harare barracks.

To the spectator it was an impressive array of disciplined soldiers, indistinguishable from each other in their camouflage uniforms and their impassive faces under green berets. It was the kind of military occasion you might witness in many parts of the world.

But there was more to it than met the eye, as the only white chaplain in the Zimbabwe Army, Alec Smith, who is attached to the Commandos, told me last week. Alec is the son of former Rhodesian Prime Minister, Ian Smith.

At independence in 1980 the decision was taken not to disband the three warring armies which had been killing each other for seven years, but to amalgamate them into one national Zimbabwean army. "We took the easy way out," jokes Alec Smith. "It would be as if just after World War II you had joined an SS Battalion with the Marines."

But it worked. And last November this parade marked the unveiling of a war memorial which consisted of a great Commando dagger pointing skyward, supported on a tripod representing the three armies. "It is a symbolic representation of what has happened," says Smith. Reconciliation had been the proclaimed policy of the new government at independence, and "if anywhere you can see reconciliation, it's in the army."

Most people at the ceremony might have just seen soldiers all looking alike, he told us, but he knew each one of them personally. He knew who had been in Mugabe's ZANLA forces, and who had been in Joshua Nkomo's ZIPRA forces, and who had been in the white-led Rhodesian army. Here they all were not only marching together but even sharing the same barracks and having adjoining beds.

"That even one soldier could be reconciled with his

enemy was amazing," says Smith. "That thousands were reconciled is a wonder." He describes seeing one former Rhodesian Army soldier wearing a T-shirt which in its humorous way underlined the extraordinary transformation which had happened. It read: "Southern African War Games 1972–1979 Second Place."

In his book, *Now I Call Him Brother* (Marshalls), Smith writes, "Many people wave an airy hand and say, 'Of course we've got an integrated army now,' without even vaguely understanding what individual people had to go through in terms of personal reorientation to achieve that unity."

Wishing to let the world know of these developments, Smith invited the Harare representative of one of the principal American TV networks to have an exclusive opportunity to film the dedication of the new war memorial. The man was naturally delighted and asked permission from his New York office to do so. Back came a telex which said in essence: We're not interested, send us some bad news. Smith was shown the telex. He cannot recall the exact wording but the words "bad news" had stayed in his mind.

It is not surprising, then, that our perceptions of Zimbabwe and maybe Africa as a whole are a bit skewed. Nor is it surprising that Smith should feel the need, while in the United States, to stress his country's positive achievements. He is well aware of the debate about what road his country should follow in the future, and the possibility that it might take a Marxist direction or become a one-party state. "This is being debated freely and openly," he said. He is aware, too, of abuses of human rights, particularly in the treatment of some of the minority Ndebele tribe. But he feels the world should know Zimbabwe's "success story."

Smith characterized the images of Africa in the United States as famine as in Ethiopia, dictatorships as in Idi Amin's Uganda, and racial conflict as in South Africa. "Zimbabwe is none of those images," he said. Despite drought conditions Zimbabwe had in most years not only fed itself but also helped feed five neighboring countries from its surplus. Last year his country exported six million dollars in food aid to Ethiopia. Race relations in Zimbabwe were better than in

most countries he had visited, including Britain; and
Zimbabwe's multi-party democracy, with five political
parties represented in Parliament, encompassed a wider
political spectrum than the U.S. Congress.

"That didn't happen by accident," he said, "but because
people decided themselves to be different and committed
themselves to make their nation different." He believes that
Zimbabwe "could probably act as a role model for peaceful
change in South Africa."

Referring to the way the media so often were obsessed
with the negative, he said, "When did you last read of the
plane that didn't crash? That's the plane I want to be on."

June 19, 1986

The unguarded Prime Minister

SAY SWEDEN and what do you think of? It could be neutrality
and Nobel prizes, or Saabs and Volvos, or Dag
Hammarskjold and Folke Bernadotte, or Ingemar Johansson
and Bjorn Borg and the new young tennis aces. Indeed,
Anders Jarryd last month became the first Swede since Borg
to win the WCT tournament. It could be the Bergmans,
Ingrid and Ingmar. It could even be, justified or not, easy
sex and suicide.

The Swedes have set a standard for the world in many
areas, whether in cradle-to-grave security or in sportsman-
ship on the tennis court. They often take a more global view
than many a larger country. Sweden, for instance, gives more
per capita to the world's poor than almost any other nation.
It is a very open, non-violent society.

So the assassination of Swedish Prime Minister Olof
Palme on a Stockholm street corner was for Swedes and

perhaps for many others more of a shock than the death of President Kennedy. *The Times* of London described him as "one of the most vibrant figures in Nordic political history," and the *Financial Times* said that the passing of no other prime minister would be quite so universally mourned." *The Guardian* editorialized, "Sweden in the Palme era never ceased to resemble a rich man with a conscience." Commonwealth Secretary-General Sridath Ramphal called him "one of the world's greatest citizens."

Palme had always refused to allow bodyguards to accompany him on private engagements, and every day he walked home from work. That he felt safe doing so even late at night without a bodyguard was, according to the *Sunday Express*, "a marvellous tribute to his country."

The shock and sadness was not because Palme was universally loved. He wasn't. At home he was often merciless to his political opponents. Abroad, he was outspoken in his condemnation of what he thought was unjust. If he appeared anti-American, he was also clearly anti-communist. But he had a bigness of heart. As Martin Linton wrote in *The Guardian*, "What has become clear since his death is that even his opponents admired and respected him." The *Sunday Express* wrote, "Even in Conservative circles there is an admission that he was in a class by himself. He represented the face of Sweden abroad as a bridge for Sweden's solidarity with deprived peoples."

In Sweden some see his most remarkable achievements as the holding together of the Social Democratic Party for fifteen years, and managing to bring down inflation and reduce unemployment to 2.5% without cutting back on welfare. But it was his world stature that produced the remarkable outpouring of tribute at his funeral and memorial service, which were attended by world leaders from 120 countries.

The whole of Sweden came to a standstill to honor Palme. At a signal from the Speaker of the Parliament, broadcast live on radio and TV, all cars and taxis and buses came to a halt, schoolchildren and factory workers stood at attention, and all work stopped in factories and stores.

At the memorial service, hosted by the Swedish Social Democratic Party in the Stockholm Town Hall, people from all strata of Swedish society and members of the Palme family were joined by guests from East and West, North and South, rich and poor nations. In the front row were members of the royal family and then, following protocol, on the left of Queen Silvia the representative of Albania and, side by side, Chancellor Helmut Kohl of the German Federal Republic and Chairman Erich Honecker of the German Democratic Republic, and Secretary of State George Shultz. In the next rows were President Chernenko of the Soviet Union, former President Nyerere of Tanzania, President Kaunda of Zambia, and Prime Minister Mugabe of Zimbabwe.

No seat had been reserved for a representative of the South African government but Desmond Tutu, Alan Boesak and Oliver Tambo, ANC leader in exile, were present. In fact, at the commemoration service in the Cathedral the next day the sermon was preached by Boesak, introduced by Tutu.

Foreign speakers at the memorial service included Indian Prime Minister Rajiv Gandhi and former German Federal Chancellor Willy Brandt, who had worked with Palme in the Brandt Commission. A choir of 284 children from all districts of Sweden sang the old canon *Dona Nobis Pacem* – Give us peace. The Swedish King, Carl XVI Gustav, told the international audience that the past weeks had proved that the ideas of Olof Palme had met with a deep response in the Swedish people's soul. "Through his decease," he said, "a Swedish voice in the world is silenced, a voice all listened to, a voice that spoke with commitment and passion against violence and oppression, and in favor of peace, freedom and justice."

Friends in Sweden wrote me that although few of the foreign guests understood the speeches in Swedish, they must have felt the spirit of reconciliation behind the words. The breadth of Palme's vision and the depth of his commitment to bring about real change in the world, they said, only dawned on many Swedes at his death. "A fresh wave of reconciliation has gone through our nation. Many have begun a reassessment of our basic values as common to all, and understood that the changing of material conditions and social structures must combine with the elimination of bitterness and hate in human attitudes."

This is another area where Sweden could set a standard for the world, becoming, as Frank Buchman, initiator of Moral Re-Armament, said nearly fifty years ago, "a reconciler of the nations." The new Swedish Prime Minister Ingvar Carlsson said, quoting Olof Palme, "There is no 'they and we', only 'we.' " A sentiment to applaud, a man to honor, on May Day.

May 1, 1986

Indian Apartheid

PRIME MINISTER Rajiv Gandhi complained recently that the United States does not appreciate India's role in world politics. If this is so, the loss is to both countries. I may well be prejudiced – I have been nine times to India, have lived in homes throughout the subcontinent and written two books about aspects of the country's life – but I do consider that it is in America's interest to make more of an effort to understand and support the world's most populous democracy. Particularly if we believe that democracy is the system of government we prefer for the world.

I was very glad to receive a letter from Congressman Stephen Solarz, from New York, in which he stated, "You know so well the importance of India to democracy and to the preservation of peace in the world. Few nations match India in stature and commitment to freedom. Few nations have made as great an effort toward peace among the superpowers as India. Few nations are as influential – and have as much future potential. You know, as well, that India does

158 *Around the globe*

not get the attention it deserves – particularly from many within the United States."

Now, Solarz's letter was not prompted from personal knowledge of me or my work. It was a fund-raising ploy to help him get re-elected. As an Englishman who chooses not to get involved in American politics and certainly not to take sides, I won't be sending money. But I will be writing to commend him, as Chairman of the House Subcommittee on Asian and Pacific Affairs, for his important support for India. This has included promoting better relations, helping remove bans on aid to India, and working to prevent a further Bhopal disaster. Solarz is currently trying to reverse a recently adopted House Foreign Affairs Committee amendment which slashed economic aid to India by 30%.

India, it is true, has a more visible profile here than when I came eight years ago. Productions like *Gandhi, Passage to India, Jewel in the Crown,* and an exhibition like last year's Indian Festival of Science, have whetted the American appetite for things Indian. Increasingly I meet Americans who have gone to see the Indian sights. India, incidentally, attracted a million tourists last year.

But too often it is tragedy, like Bhopal, and other bad news, like the Hindu-Sikh killings and the travails of Rajiv Gandhi's government, which get the attention. And a visit to Moscow of an Indian leader or to India of a Soviet leader, and arms purchases from the Soviet Union, are reported without the context which helps an American appreciate what non-alignment means.

I recently had the chance to interview one of India's outstanding figures, Rajmohan Gandhi. He is a grandson of Mahatma Gandhi and of C. Rajagopalachari, first Indian Governor General of independent India, both men in the forefront of the struggle for freedom achieved 40 years ago.

Like his distinguished grandfathers, Rajmohan has a dedication to helping India surmount its problems. He wants to see Indians deal with the "unfinished business' of the Mahatma's revolution. He is heartened by India's material progress where, as he says, India is now able to feed itself, and has the capacity to manufacture almost everything it needs. But he is sometimes frustrated by the "enormous" problems: "In a hospital you have more patients than beds, in a bus more people than seats, in a home more people than it can accommodate."

He is proud of the scientists, doctors, surgeons, and nurses the country produces, and the success in life they have made in many parts of the world. He admires the resilience of the Indian people and their capacity to adjust to suffering: "The poorer an Indian is, the more he has suffered, the quicker he is to make room for somebody else." But he is affronted by his country's failure to progress further in reconciling Indians of different religions and castes with each other. "We in India continue our conflicts over decades, over centuries. The time has come to end this chapter."

Gandhi, like his Gandhi grandfather, believes in the need for a revolution of character. "Self-centeredness is the great bane in our country." He wants to attack the cruelty and hypocrisy he feels is in the Indian nature: "The Indian character has to change from cruelty to kindness." For instance, he says, India, while urging the Front Line states in Africa to end relations with South Africa, continues its own diamond trade. And his country, while condemning apartheid, practices its own apartheid in the way it treats the former "untouchables:" "Unless we tackle this in our country in all its manifestations, how can we really say we have the answer for apartheid?"

He also has a dream of a new India, a "beautiful India," which is clean ethically, morally, and to the eyes, with an end to hunger and thirst and lack of housing as well as to violence, and with an end to conflict with Pakistan. He has taken a number of initiatives in these areas, the latest to write a book, *Eight Lives* (SUNY), which is about great Muslim figures in the subcontinent and is the fruit of his work as a Wilson Fellow in Washington, DC. "It's a conscious attempt," he says, "towards bridgebuilding between the Hindus and the Muslims."

I asked him what he would like to see from the United States. "I would ask," he replied, "that America does realize that, great and wonderful and important as America is,

America is not the world. I would also say that America needs to have real faith in what she says she believes in, what Lincoln said he believed in – freedom, care, compassion, equality, in God we trust, the moral content of social life."

Gandhi fears that Americans now seem to be losing their faith in these powerful engines of change, these foundations of our society. "If America could recall the truths on which she was founded," he told me, "and make a genuine commitment to those truths, and then say that those truths are needed for the world as a whole, America would then have so much to give."

August 13, 1987

Waiting to die

MY FAMILY has over the years had many links with Jamaica. My father used to go there regularly in the days when the banana boat was the means of travel, and as I was growing up we often had Jamaicans staying with us. So I was very grateful to have had the chance recently to visit this Caribbean island for the first time.

As it happened while I was there I met a remarkable cross section of Jamaicans, including most of the cabinet. But one of the most impressive people was Woody Mitchell. Woody helps direct a multi-faceted "cottage industry" that includes exporting to the US, Canada, and Britain – and he does it all without a telephone (the one in the village doesn't work) and from a wheelchair.

His story is exceptional both because he has triumphed over disaster and because his village of Walkerswood, where I stayed, is becoming a model of community-based development. Indeed, the government minister responsible for Social

Development told me, "Whenever you talk about community development, you talk about Walkerswood."

As you climb into the hills above the tourist town of Ocho Rios, negotiating the winding curves of Fern Gully, you come across this attractive farming community of between two and three thousand people. Across from the Community Center and its sports field and the post office is a café, craft shops, general store, woodworking shop and Woody's office.

This development has been made possible by a combination of enlightened racial attitudes among white and black, a nurturing of "grassroots" democracy, and an honesty of leadership that has given confidence to foreign aid donors. A foundation of faith, too, may account for the readiness of many in the community, when disputes arise which have racial or political undertones, to seek for what is right rather than their own interest. The village spirit and the creation of local jobs has meant that, contrary to the trend in Jamaica, the drift to the cities has been slowed.

It was during the building of the Community Center that Woody's interest was engaged. Shortly before, Woody had been paralyzed by a traffic accident in Kingston, the capital. "I was turned upside down," he told me. "All my dreams went out of the window. I was waiting to die." But thanks to his family who visited him daily over months, to others in wheelchairs, to reading books about people like Helen Keller who had overcome their disabilities, he began to realize "it wasn't the end of the world."

When he came out of hospital he began to participate, with his parents, in community work in Walkerswood. "The community was so motivated," he remembers. "On three Saturdays we put in the floor of the Walkerswood Center, laying 40 by 90 feet of concrete. And we built it for J$10,000, J$1800 under cost." It was in Walkerswood, too, that he met his wife, Pat, who had also suffered in an accident. Getting to know Woody gave her a lift. "It got her to stop moping around," he says with a laugh.

It has been said that a Jamaican sees a problem to every solution. If that is true, and if the assessments of Walkerswood as a model for development are true, Woody is a true Jamaican. For the inadequacies of the community loom large in his mind. When I talked with him he was wrestling with such matters as missing customs papers from a shipment of seasoning which had just arrived in England, and the theft of a battery which operates the satellite communication system linking the village school with other schools and communities in the South Pacific.

He also expressed disappointment that more people were not stepping forward. "The hope was that the more we employed people on community projects, the more the numbers would swell at meetings," he says. "No such thing happened." The more people got, the more they expected. They didn't always pull their weight. Woody is sad that because of his cottage industry responsibilities he doesn't have the same time and energy he previously had to devote to community affairs. He hopes, however, that his example will give courage to others, particularly to those disabled by accident.

A report in Jamaica's daily, *The Gleaner*, said that the "miracle at Walkerswood" was in the spirit of the people there and reflected initiative and community enterprise rarely paralleled in Jamaica. "In a country debilitated by multiple divisions, jealousies and suspicions, they have retained their common sense," the paper writes. "The result is that all classes and ages have been able to work together."

Walkerswood has demonstrated, as another Jamaican saying goes, that "it takes two hands to clap."

May 12, 1988

Christianity of obedience

WE SOMETIMES FORGET that South Africa is not just an issue, it is people, people who are no better and no worse than we are. Each South African, like each one of us, faces daily moral choices. Let me tell you about the choices made by one of them, a farmer, Roland Kingwill. He comes from the Karoo, an area of hard arid land resembling a semi-desert, where it takes five acres of grazing to sustain one sheep.

I first met Roly more than thirty years ago, some time after he had decided to tackle three crucial issues in his country – race relations, soil erosion and unemployment. In a new video, *Promise of the Veld*, he describes what has happened as a result.

As a nominal Christian, he says, he was confronted with the idea, "God has a plan, you have a part." From that day a new land ethic began to grow in him, that the soil belongs to God and to future generations. He was exploiting it for his own gain and, in fact, believes that had he continued in the old way the farm would have died.

Was he willing, he asked himself, to put his life entirely under God's direction, not knowing where it would lead? He decided to rise even earlier one morning to sit quiet and listen. "God," he said, "if you can speak, speak to me now." Immediately, he recalls, he got the clear thought, "You must get going. I have work for you."

Each morning he would take time to discover what that work would be. He knew the place to start was with himself and his farm. He thought about the deterioration of the land. His farm was dependent on a spring. Grass on the upland held the rainwater as it seeped into the earth and emerged as a fountain. If the grass were destroyed the water would rush away and the spring would die. But wool was the main source of income and he was putting all the sheep on the farm he could.

The thought came with startling clarity: "Reduce your stock by one third. Institute a system of rotational grazing." It was, as he said, asking an awful lot. But he was committed to the Christianity of obedience. He sold a third of his stock, and cut his income by a third. The years that followed were difficult. They had to cut out every luxury. But gradually grass began to grow where there had been no grass before. Slowly sheep began to produce more wool per head and the lambing increased. Cattle began to feed where there had been no feed before.

"Our values began to change," he says. "Now our wealth was not in our bank account but in the health of our livestock and the density of our *veld* cover." New ideas flourished. Scientists and extension officers came to see. When Roly took these radical steps little had been proven in this field or was even known. He was invited first to speak to and then join the soil conservation committee.

Side by side with this new awareness of the land grew a new awareness of all South Africa's people. "I am deeply conscious," he says, "that I am part of an unjust structure of white privilege. This has got to change. It will change." Roly began with himself. He realized that he expected his workers to be at the *kraal* gate at sunrise ready to work. They had to obey, with no argument. In his morning quiet time he thought he should apologize to them for his white arrogance. He hesitated, delayed, thought this was going too far. What would his neighbors say? But he was committed to obedience. So he did it. And he discovered very quickly that his dictatorial manner had stifled creativity. His color categorization had put a ceiling on people and what they could do. Now each individual on the farm, and how they lived, became important to him.

He improved their housing and, quite unheard of at that time, provided a school and paid for teachers. Today farm schools are subsidized, and teachers are paid by the government.

Another clear thought in his morning quiet time was to give his staff a sense of security. He had kept the right to instant dismissal. "No one who wants to work will be dismissed," he told them, "even if times get hard." Their homes would be theirs as long as they wanted to stay. "I began to see," he says in the video, "how much pride and convention had walled me off from other races. It was the beginning of a new era. Our lives have been enriched."

When there was drought in the area it was a particularly hard time for the farmers. Then the bankers and economists would come and advise them to operate with the minimum number of staff and fire the rest. But Roly and his family had decided to put people before profit and also to see what they could do to combat unemployment. His son, David, says, "We feel the right place to start is with the needs of people. Instead of seeing how few we could run the farm with, we decided to operate on the basis of how many we could support on the farm. It's not easy on the pocket, but the result is a happy staff. We have people who are up to the fourth generation on the farm."

Members of the family have also created employment for black rural women, training them to do leather and sheepskin work. They've helped start a weaving industry, which now is exporting its products.

At the end of the video Roly sums up his experience; "I did decide to lay down my right to my life, to do what I want, where I want, how I want. I did not find ease or comfort or prosperity, but a purpose, a deep joy, and a great hope, and I have proved that when man listens, God speaks, when man obeys, God acts. It is not a question of white domination, not black domination, but black and white together listening to the father of us all and walking shoulder to shoulder as sons and daughters of God towards a great future for us all."

In an article earlier this year in a South African paper, Roly Kingwill wrote, "Maybe there are whites who believe that some simple compromise in our present constitution and other structures will bring change, security, and cooperation to our divided society. That hope is false. For complete cure of our sickness, we must accept the full treatment, and it will be painful to start with; but after full healing, our future will be great and rewarding. If we have the courage to put right all that is wrong within ourselves and in our nation, this southern tip of Africa will make a lasting and honored contribution to all Africa, and even to the world."

One should not despair about the future of South Africa when there are families like the Kingwills at work.

August 28, 1986

Halos rust easily

1985 MAY GO DOWN as the year of an Irish pop singer, a gaunt, unkempt, rough-tongued humanitarian called Bob Geldof. For his awkward, angular figure came to represent both the extent of the world's worst tragedy and the hope of overcoming it and, as the London *Daily Telegraph* wrote, "a great return to the power of personal conscience to affect large issues." He has been nominated for the Nobel Peace Prize.

Bob, himself, has no delusions. Told that someone had referred to him as "Saint Bob," he responded, "I don't want to be St. Bob because halos get heavy and they rust very easily, and I know I have feet of clay because my socks stink. I don't live up to it and I'm not interested in living up to it." He compares his Band Aid organization to a shooting star, "brilliant and beautiful for a second and then living forever in your memory."

History will ask of us, he believes, how a world which was burning food, storing it, letting it rot, could watch starvation on television and say, "That's all right." He had simply "tried to create an international lobby of concern that would affect nearly all governments." And it came about just because he happened to be at home the night the plight of the Ethiopian people was shown on British television.

A reputedly cynical Australian journalist, Phillip Adams, describes in *The Weekend Australian* how an exhausted and bitter Geldof "vanquished a room full of egos" at the annual broadcasting award ceremonies in Melbourne. "Geldof," writes Adams, "made what was quite simply the most affecting speech I've ever heard. And it made me wonder what would happen if, after all, Jesus Christ did have that long-awaited Second Coming. Frankly, I don't think we'd treat him any better this time round. Among too many people, including me, the tendency to be suspicious of Geldof and his enormous efforts was based on a reluctance to examine our own motives and, insofar as they survive, our ideals. We resented him because he made so many of us feel morally shabby."

It was Geldof's inspiration that assembled the "global jukebox," 52 performers in Britain, the United States and the Soviet Union linked together for a 16-hour concert that was beamed by 14 international satellites to 500 million TV sets and an estimated 1.5 billion people in 169 nations. 72,000 people, including the Prince and Princess of Wales, attended the Live Aid performance at Wembley, with 90,000 at JFK stadium in Philadelphia. Over $60 million was raised for famine relief.

Britain's *Sunday Mirror* believes that the response of ordinary people in all countries proved that goodness and decency can still triumph over hatred, oppression and terrorism. If the leaders of the world, the paper wrote, were tuned into Live Aid, they heard more than the beat of rock music. They heard the hearts of all the people saying that our planet can be made a better place for us all to share.

Over the months Geldof has worked to keep awareness of what he calls "the African holocaust" alive, to cut through obstacles that prevent aid getting to the starving, to confront heartlessness in government. For instance, his assault on the "constipated EEC bureaucracy" for accumulating mountains of food while Africans starve was, according to *The Observer*, exactly what millions of people would have liked to have had the chance to say themselves. "Do They Know It's Christmas," Band Aid's fund-raising record, was at the top of the charts. And School Aid, Sport Aid, and many other initiatives have been sparked. Now Geldof and his organization are sifting proposals and consulting with experts on the best use of the money raised, dividing it roughly 40% for emergency and 60% for long-term needs.

Some two million people died from starvation in Ethiopia and the Sudan in 1985, and despite the rains in many parts of drought-stricken Africa the crisis remains acute and requires a united international strategy to meet it. Urgent support is needed, for instance, to help small farmers with their agricultural projects, to build bridges and roads and small irrigation schemes, to arrange conferences in Africa where solutions can be identified and long-term planning put in hand.

"The only way to deal with the problem," says Geldof, in an interview in *Rolling Stone*, "is to deal with it perhaps on the scale of a Marshall Plan for Africa." To mount something of that order calls for courage from our legislators and support from their constituents.

For years our governments have seemed to operate on the basis that there are no votes in aid and development. The response to Bob and his fellow rock musicians may have proved otherwise. Let us for the sake of the idealism of our young people, and the lives of millions in the developing world, hope that this is so.

January 2, 1986

When did you last steal?

AFRICA has lost a statesman and our family a long-time friend in the death at the age of 78 of Alhaji Yakubu Tali, Tolon Na, of Ghana. Tolon Na had been Ambassador, Member of Parliament, Deputy Speaker of the National Assembly, and for many years President of the Northern Territories Council. He was, according to the *Daily Graphic* of Accra, "one of the most remarkable personalities Northern Ghana has ever produced."

A devout Muslim and respected Chief of his people, he believed in the importance of integrity and faith in God. "In Africa," he once said, "we need a way of life based on accepting what God wants. It means crossing my will with God's. That is the root of Islam which means submission to God." Shortly before his death he wrote, "Allah, I know, has a solution to every problem, providing we listen long enough for his direction."

In the home of my brother, Gerald, and his wife, Judith, there is a lovely piece of Kente cloth, the colorful material so typical of Ghana. It was a wedding present from Tolon Na. Gerald has spent much of his life in West Africa and first got to know Tolon Na in 1954. I have a photo of my brother taken in front of Tolon Na's home near Tamale in Northern Ghana. Gerald remembers the occasion well. "While we were sitting talking about our friends around the world, under the canopy outside his palace where he would give his elders and people audience," Gerald writes, "he suddenly jumped up in the middle of a sentence and came out with a gun. Apparently he had noticed a hawk that was after his chickens.

"I also remember the gift of food we were given to take on our journey. It is tradition in that part of Ghana that if one does not stay for a meal one is given a gift of food to take. As I bade farewell first to his mother, then to Tolon Na, and finally to Tali Na, his brother in the neighboring village, each gave me a gift. Driving away I discovered I had two live guinea fowl, a yam, and 101 eggs. As I was driving 700 miles in the heat I took the eggs to the local rest house to be hard-boiled."

In a letter to Gerald a while back, Tolon Na reminded him of the dinner he had with our parents in our home in London in 1960, when he was on the way to the UN. He also recalled the day he came to Gerald's home in Accra with the whole front bench, that is the whole leadership, of the Opposition in the Ghana Parliament. Gerald is hardly likely to forget that occasion, either, as he was having a siesta when the phalanx of robed and turbaned Muslim dignitaries arrived at the door unannounced. Tolon Na wanted them to hear of Moral Re-Armament's worldwide work for reconciliation. He particularly asked Gerald to tell the story of how the initiator of Moral Re-Armament, Frank Buchman, had helped transform the spirit at Penn State University through the change in the life of the bootlegger, the agnostic dean, and the most popular student.

Tolon Na's own encounter with Buchman led to dramatic change also. He was attending a session at the Moral Re-Armament conference center at Caux, Switzerland in 1954. The Africans present were on the platform. A speaker referred to stealing, and what it cost the nation. Buchman, who was sitting near Tolon Na, turned to him with a smile and said, "When did you last steal?"

"This struck me like a depth-charge," the Ghanaian leader said later. "I could not answer it there and then, not even immediately afterwards. I retired to my room and lay on my bed and prayed to Allah to take me into his loving care, repenting for all the evils I had done since childhood. As I lay there by myself I felt God was still waiting for a reply. I saw the whole world watching. It was the greatest challenge that I had ever faced."

Tolon Na wrote down all the times he had stolen. "The idea tore my mind from the grip of my former self," he said. He decided to make restitution and to apologize to people whom he had wronged, and to "accept the rule of God in my heart in all that I do or say at home and abroad."

The experience set him off on a road that affected his country. He is credited with preserving the unity of Ghana when the Northern Region was in danger of seceding, probably saving the country from civil war. When High Commissioner to Nigeria he stood up to his leader, Kwame Nkrumah, when he feared that an action by the Prime Minister would jeopardize relations between the two countries. "I was scared to do it," he said, "But I realized that it is the way some of us live that makes our leaders dictators. We tell them what will please them to gain promotion or other favors." Later, when the military took over, they asked him to stay on as Ghana's representative in Nigeria, because they recognized his integrity.

Speaking at the conference in Caux some years ago, Tolon Na said, "We have always blamed the Constitution when things go wrong. We have had four since independence and the fifth is being drafted. But the fault lies not there. It lies in Ghanaians. The troubles are of our own making. If the leaders change they can change their people. If the people change they can change their leaders. A combination of both can work together to bring peace to our continent. In Africa we need a way of life based on accepting what God wants. I am allowing God to rule my life so I can rid myself of pride, hate and selfishness, and live to affect my nation and the world."

Tolon Na's life was a demonstration of what can happen when men in political life decide to do that. It is also a confirmation that Christians and Muslims can work together for the advance of faith in the world.

Tolon Na's grandson was recently in Gerald's home, and told him that he often found his grandfather studying the Bible. Tolon Na once said to a friend of mine, "You're a Christian, I'm a Muslim. Will you answer me two questions? When I let God's thoughts rule my mind, I am experiencing the Holy Spirit? Right? When I know that God's will crosses my will, and I choose God's will, I experience the Cross? Right?"

I'm no theologian, but it makes sense to me.

September 25, 1986

9 Back to basics

A couple of years ago a computer failure in Brussels knocked out typesetting capabilities at a Belgian daily newspaper. A 32-page edition duly appeared the next morning – entirely handwritten. The Belgian journalists, fortunately, still knew how to put pen to paper. A photo of the tabloid's front page was captioned in my local paper, "Back to the basics."

Our society has to deal with a lot more than the possibility of computer failure, though that gets increasingly scarier. The old order steadily gives way. If, as we now learn, dinosaurs may have evolved into birds, if Brooks Brothers is British, the Bank of California Japanese, Alka-Seltzer German, if even spinach can be bad for you, are there any certainties left?

Familiar landmarks crumble or are removed. The moral fences along the road of life are overgrown and scarcely recognizable. Some of the road signs have been reversed. Is there a moral database for our personal computers?

Mass cheating

I HAD a hubcap stolen from my car the other day. Most annoying. And I was appalled to discover what it would cost to replace it. I have insurance against vandalism, but because of the deductible only half the cost of replacing the hubcap is covered.

I mentioned this to a garage mechanic and he said, "Why don't you tell the insurance company that all four hubcaps were stolen, and that would cover it."

There's a parking lot downtown which I sometimes use. On my last visit the attendant, no doubt wishing to be helpful, accepted payment for an hour but wrote a larger sum on my receipt, obviously expecting me to use it to claim reimbursement.

I wonder what dishonesty costs the nation and whether there is any moral difference between petty fiddling on the part of the lowly citizen and major deceit at a national level, and, indeed, whether we can have any authority to tackle the larger issues unless we are straight ourselves.

I notice that columnist Ellen Goodman is writing about such matters.

In an article in the *Washington Post* headed "Surrounded by lies," she details seventeen common lies she might encounter in a day, ranging from being told that Mr. Blank she wants to speak to is "in a meeting" to the response "the computer is down," when neither excuse happens to be true.

She was brought out of her usual adult stupor into a state of high consciousness, she says, by what she calls the Disinformation Brigade at the White House. She suggests that many of us have "grown terminally tolerant of 'mis-' and 'dis-' information."

"The sociologists," she goes on, "will tell you that government lying destroys the fabric of public trust. But as I sit here waiting for Mr. Blank, I harbor a reverse theory: that the fabric of everyday lying is the perfect environment for ripening the government lie."

What we need, says Ellen Goodman, is "a daily dose of

intolerance for falsehood. We need to get unused to being lied to. To call people on the little ones." "I, for one," she concludes, "am going to begin with Mr. Blank. Today. Just as soon as he gets out of his meeting."

This question of dishonesty is a universal one, and in every country reversing it requires the same readiness of the individual to develop that intolerance for falsehood. It so happens that I have just received a related story from India, from a young man, Rahul Kapadia, who is at present studying film-making in Britain.

Rahul was one day challenged by the thought, "As I am, so is my nation." It made him aware for the first time what his cheating in exams meant for his country. Before that he had always prided himself on being a good cheater who never got caught. Now, he didn't look forward to one day being treated by a doctor with an unearned certificate. He apologized to his school principal and decided never to cheat again. He soon rose to the top of his class.

A few years later, in 1982, he took his final school exams. He was amazed by the "mass" cheating which went on. There were 600 students divided into classrooms with two supervisors in each. When the three-hour exam started, the various supervisors closed the doors and permitted the students to cheat, letting them use dictionaries and calculators even though these were specifically forbidden, even helping them themselves. One supervisor would station himself at the door to warn if the chief supervisor were coming.

Rahul complained to the chief supervisor, with the result that at his final paper six thugs pushed him around, and two supervisors threatened to tear up his paper and mark him absent. He managed to complete the exam but was disappointed with the result.

Air Chief Marshal I. H. Latif, the Governor of Maharashtra, the Indian State in which Rahul lived, who was also the Chancellor of all the universities there, heard about this experience and asked Rahul to come and see him. He went along with other students who had decided not to cheat. The first thing the Governor said to them was, "I cannot believe there are students in Bombay who are not cheating in exams." He asked the students for their suggestions, keeping them talking for over 40 minutes.

Within the next ten months the Governor met with every University Vice-Chancellor in the State, and by the time of the next year's examinations the newspapers were writing about the drop in cheating. Exams were held on time, results declared promptly, and universities and colleges opened when they were supposed to, whereas the previous year there had been a two-month delay because of the cheating and subsequent reexaminations that were required. The newspapers paid tribute to the Governor as the one responsible for the anti-cheating drive. He said, "If it wasn't for the students who came to see me, I as Governor and Chancellor would not have known what steps to take because I wasn't sure of student support."

The Governor is now Indian Ambassador to France. But, as Rahul says, "The battle still goes on." In February this year the daughter of the Chief Minister of the State was wrongly passed in her medical exams. Another student, who failed, filed a case about the daughter in the Bombay High Court. The Chief Minister put pressure on the new Chancellor to get the case withdrawn. The Chancellor, in turn, tried to pressure the Vice-Chancellor but he refused to act and resigned.

The High Court verdict implicated the Chief Minister who then resigned on orders from Prime Minister Rajiv Gandhi. Later the new Governor had to resign because of the part he, too, played in trying to quash the case.

A little honesty earlier in the day would certainly have saved a lot of time and money.

November 13, 1986

Setting a murderer free

NICK WAS A MURDERER. A Christmas experience helped set him on a new course.

A friend of mine, Denis Foss, was captain of a cargo ship that plied from Baltic ports to the Mediterranean.

On one trip, Denis, having to find a second steward in a hurry, signed on a much-scarred applicant, Nick.

It was only after sailing that he discovered that Nick had just come out of prison for committing a murder in Paris, had committed another in Antwerp, and been guilty of further violent crimes. Denis said to Nick, "You have paid the price as far as the law is concerned and you are now a free man. If I hear you have told anyone I will put you ashore. Now go and get on with your job."

On the voyage Nick, though morose, did his work well. And Denis took the time to listen to his life story and help him be really honest about the past.

Nick described to Denis how he had been a convinced Hitler Youth whose parents were Belgian Nazis. As a teenager he volunteered for the German forces attacking Russia and was badly wounded at Stalingrad. When he got home at the end of the war his home had been blown up by the communist underground and all his family killed.

With no home and no training he turned to a career of raiding small post offices. At one place an old lady resisted; he hit her over the head, and later she died. The police eventually caught him, he told Denis, and he spent eight years in prison. Then he got a job as a steward on a Panamanian ship. On shore in Hawaii some of the crew found themselves without money to get back to ship. "I know how to get money," said Nick, "we'll hold up a post office." The American police picked them up and shipped them home. This time Nick served eighteen months.

In Paris a man offered him a wad of notes if he would sleep with him. "Go away," said Nick, "I've seen too much of that in prison. I hate it." But as he walked away he thought to himself, "Why should that dirty old man have all that money and I've got nothing." He described how he picked up a brick and threw it, knocking the man down, dead. Denis interrupted, "Did throwing the brick kill him or did you pick up the brick afterwards and kill him deliberately?" "I hit him afterward," Nick admitted.

Once more Nick went back to jail. But luckily he met a chaplain who had faith in him. This man advertized for a Christian family who would adopt a twice convicted murderer. When Nick came out of his second eight-year term they took him into their home. He had been with them just a few weeks when he joined ship.

As they were sailing across the Bay of Biscay, Nick asked Denis for money to buy a radio in Algiers. "It's a good idea but don't you think," said Denis, referring to the post offices, "that you ought to make some restitution." "I don't see why I should do a thing like that," Nick responded. It was just before Christmas.

On British merchant ships it is the custom at Christmas dinner that after the officers have eaten, the stewards then sit down and are served by the officers. When a menu was placed in front of Nick he suddenly rushed off. Denis found him weeping in his cabin. "Always I have been pushed around. Always been ordered to do things. Always at the bottom of the tree, and then to have one of the senior officers come up to me and say, 'What would you like, sir?' was more than I could take," he told his captain. Nick rejoined the table – and from that moment his attitude to people and to life changed.

In January he listed all the places he had robbed, and how much he had stolen, and started mailing money back. He began visiting police chiefs in the different ports, and they in turn began coming to the ship to tell the captain of the remarkable change in one of his crew. "I feel I must use my experiences and what I've learned from being on board this ship to help the police deal with murderers," explained Nick. "If they could learn that it's possible to change the attitude of murderers, it could be a most heartening thing."

Through his adopted family Denis kept in touch with Nick who continued his career on other ships, rising to

Chief Steward. They wrote to Denis to say that Nick was miraculously different, that he was a great help to the family, greatly loved by all. Suddenly Nick's health broke down. Wounds suffered at Stalingrad caught up with him and he died, in his mid-forties.

"In my bedroom," says Denis, "is a picture Nick gave me when he left my ship. It shows a seaman steering a ship in rough weather with the sea blowing over him. Behind him is the shadowy image of Christ. As Nick gave it to me, he said, 'I believe that Christ has been guiding this ship and the people in it and made me totally different. I'm eternally grateful, and I want you to keep this and remember me.' "

December 19, 1985

Jack Anderson's discovery

INVESTIGATIVE JOURNALIST Jack Anderson has uncovered something unusual, at least unusual for his column. It is the institution of a quiet hour in the offices of the US and Foreign Commercial Service of the Commerce Department in Washington, DC.

Anderson reported in his column that the man who dreamed up the quiet hour is Kenn George, the head of the Commercial Service. George said he tried it out himself for several weeks and it worked.

According to an internal memo, says Anderson, the purpose of the quiet hour is to provide uninterrupted time to all employees so that they may do individual work, such as reading, writing, typing, proofing, etc. "The hour will not be used for meetings, conferences, telephone calls, personal business, coffee breaks, etc."

All people who normally do business with the Commercial Service will be advised not to call or visit between 3 and 4 pm. One person will take messages and advise callers that the person they are seeking is not available at the moment and will return the call shortly. Exceptions will be kept to the minimum.

Jack Anderson says that his assistant can attest to George's commitment to an afternoon quiet time because he "didn't return his call until after 4 pm."

The afternoon quiet time is a new idea. As regular listeners to my weekly talk know, I recounted last year the experience with morning quiet times of the accounting department of the Continental Telephone Company in California. And I went on from that commercial and secular experience, designed to help the busy office person step back a moment from the pressures of the day, to talk about the value of a quiet time for finding God's whispers for our lives.

As a result of that talk I received a number of letters commending the idea of starting the day with a quiet time. In fact, I even received three booklets on the subject.

One is entitled *Seven minutes with God – How To Plan a Daily Quiet Time* published by the Navigators. This would probably appeal to those who can't contemplate the full hour in the morning encouraged by some. The author, Robert D. Foster, calls it a daily "seven-up."

Foster describes how a group of students coined the slogan "Remember the morning watch" back in 1882 at Cambridge University. Their practice of taking time alone with God led, he said, to "a remarkable period of religious blessing." One of the students, Thornton, was rather lazy and invented an automatic foolproof contraption set up by his bed to get him up: "The vibration of an alarm clock set fishing tackle in motion, and the sheets, clipped to the line, moved swiftly into the air off the sleeper's body."

Call it what you want, writes Foster, quiet time, personal devotions, morning watch, or individual worship, it is the golden thread that ties every great man of God together – from Moses to David Livingstone, the prophet Amos to Billy Graham – rich and poor, businessmen and military personnel. "Every man who ever became somebody for God has this at the core of his priorities: time alone with God."

There is a catch in Foster's "seven-up." "Very soon you will discover," he writes, "that it is impossible to spend only seven minutes with the Lord. An amazing thing happens – seven minutes becomes 20, and it's not long before you're spending 30 precious minutes with him."

The second booklet I have is called *Quiet Times for Christian Growth* put out by the Intervarsity Press. It is a collection of eight weeks of readings and prayers. In the preface it says, "God's blessings are most fully realized in the person who works at delighting in God's law. His deepest blessings are not given to those wanting 'instant' godliness but to those who are willing to discipline themselves to spend time with the Lord. Regular, daily, quality quiet times of Bible study, prayer, and meditation take discipline. God then makes us fruitful disciples."

The booklet underlines that good quiet times, like everything else, take practice and discipline. "Don't be afraid to innovate," it says. "Since these are your personal times with God you can count on him being flexible enough to meet your needs in ways unique to you. Ask others about their quiet times and try a variety of techniques, but be sure to give each a fair try and a thorough evaluation."

The third booklet is called *Martin Luther's Quiet Time* (Trobisch). It is based on Luther's answer to his barber who asked the famous doctor of theology one day, "Dr. Luther, how do you pray?" Next week I'll tell you what Luther wrote.

January 23, 1986

Lasers of the spirit

A FRIEND OF MINE was talking to a senior communist official
in Eastern Europe about the practice of taking time each day
to listen to your conscience, to the inner voice, to those
promptings that can help you tell right from wrong, and
even distinguish between two courses which might both be
right. Like most of us the communist found the concept a
bit strange. But he was intrigued. "I see," he said, "it's like
a detector of truth for mankind."

The remarkable thing about these lasers of the spirit is
that they can get through to anyone. Whether you're a
believer or not, whether you are in a free society or a closed
one, whether you are brilliant or illiterate, the unexpected
thought can penetrate, and illumine, and, if acted on, transform life. An American Jewish trade unionist, explaining the
idea to a Japanese worker, called the experience "a light
going on in your head."

Last week I was speaking about the value of taking time
in quiet, undisturbed minutes in the day when you can step
back, get perspective, and be alert for inspiration. Some
people call it two-way prayer. I mentioned that Martin
Luther's barber once asked him, "Dr. Luther, how do you
pray?"

"Dear Master Peter," Luther responded, "A good clever
barber must have his thoughts, mind, and eyes concentrated
upon the razor and the beard, and not forget where he is in
his stroke and shave. If he keeps on talking or looking around
or thinking of something else, he is likely to cut a man's
mouth or nose – or even his throat. How much more must
prayer possess the heart exclusively and completely if it is to
be a good prayer."

Luther stressed the importance of taking time at the start
of the day. "It is a good thing to let prayer be the first
business in the morning and the last in the evening," he
wrote. And in the course of his forty-page letter he counselled
Master Peter to have his quiet time with pen and paper at
hand to note down what God told him. "If the Holy Spirit

should come and begin to preach to your heart, giving you rich and enlightened thoughts, then give him the honor, let your preconceived ideas go, be quiet and listen to him who can talk better than you; and note what he proclaims and write it down, so you will experience miracles."

I find writing down my thoughts helpful; it clears my mind to receive more thoughts, and then later I can check to see what happened to them. A French professor, Father Alphonse Gratry, describing the practice of taking time in silence, said over a hundred years ago, "Just take care not to lose what you hear in such times. Don't pride yourself on your memory. It is necessary to write. Write for God and for yourself. Write in order to hear the word in you, and to keep his words. If you truly are his disciples then the inspiration which comes will be most concrete, most precise, most relevant."

Sometimes, when we don't seem to be getting such concrete direction in our quiet times, it may be because we have had thoughts we have not carried out, or we have matters that need to be put right. If you woke up this morning and couldn't get KBOO on your radio, I hope you would not say, "Oh, KBOO is not broadcasting." But rather, "There's something wrong with my radio. Perhaps it needs a new battery." So it is that there may be things in us that need to be replaced if we are to be good listeners.

One who took this early morning quiet time seriously every day of his life, even in prison camp, was Eric Liddell, whose story is dramatized in *Chariots of Fire*. You may remember that at the end of the film you see on the screen: "Eric Liddell, missionary, died in occupied China at the end of World War II. All of Scotland mourned."

Last year a book by Liddell was published for the first time, *The Disciplines of the Christian Life* (Abingdon). In it he recommends setting aside specific, unhurried time each day for prayer and Bible study. "We should come to it in an honest spirit, prepared to face the challenge of God's word as it lays down a way of life," he writes, "and prepared to face any inconsistencies in our lives which make them un-Christlike."

Liddell lists suggestions how to make the most of such time. He recommends that we ask God what new responsibilities he wants us to accept today in the light of his love and the world's need. "Find out his plan. Make notes of things he wants you to do, people to pray for, etc." He asks us to accept Christ into our life for today" with all his qualities of outgoing love, honesty, purity, and unselfishness, and with his passion to do God's will."

For Liddell, obedience to God's will is the secret of spiritual knowledge and insight. "If in the quiet of your heart you feel something should be done," he writes, "stop and consider whether it is in line with the character and teaching of Jesus. If it is, obey that impulse to do it, and in doing so you will find it was God guiding you. Every Christian should live a God-guided life. If you are not guided by God, you will be guided by someone or something else. The Christian who hasn't the sense of guidance in life is missing something vital."

January 30, 1986

Through enemy lines

GEORGE SELDES, in his 487-page volume, *The Great Thoughts* (Ballantine), which I happen to be reading at the moment, includes in the index just four references to the subject of prayer, three of them negative. The book's subtitle describes the contents as "the ideas that have shaped the history of the world." The omission says more about Seldes than it does about the importance of prayer. The paucity of reference does, however, reflect the fact that in some people's lexicon prayer does not rate highly.

I mention this because next Monday Pope John Paul II

has called world religious leaders together in Assisi to pray for peace. He has also appealed to all parties involved in conflicts around the world to observe, at least during the entire day of October 27, a complete truce.

The Pope said he had launched the appeal because he believes in the value and spiritual efficacy of symbols. The truce, he said, would also stimulate people at war to reflect "on the motives which push them to seek by force, with its entourage of human miseries, that which they could obtain by sincere negotiations and by recourse to other means offered by law." Acceptance by political and military leaders in nations and groups involved in armed conflict would be a recognition that "violence does not have the last word in relations between men and nations."

More than 150 leaders of eleven major world religions are expected to participate in a program that includes prayer, fasting, and a final common meal. They range from the Archbishop of Canterbury to the Dalai Lama. With them will be representatives of Africa's traditional or animist religions. "Nothing like this has ever happened in the history of mankind," according to chief Vatican spokesman Joaquin Navarro-Vals.

Launching the idea of a day of prayer last February the Pope said, "Wars can be decided by just a few people, but peace requires the strong commitment of all." He had chosen Assisi because it was the 13th century birthplace of St. Francis who "transformed the place into a center of universal fraternity."

Last year, despite the decline elsewhere in Italy of summer tourism, the number of visitors to Assisi was up 20%. Two million visitors accompanied the brown-robed monks who led tours of the city in ten languages and combined art, history, and the Franciscan message. Modern-day Assisi in a remarkable way seems to evoke for visitors the spirit of St. Francis.

The saint's dedication to a truly Christ-centered life, with a regard for all creatures and for the environment, his own transformation from wealth and party-going to a life of poverty and selflessness, drew thousands to his side over 700 years ago, and continues to inspire millions today. His "Lord, make me an instrument of thy peace" probably adorns more American walls than any other prayer.

St. Francis was also a peacemaker in the Middle East. While the political establishment of his day was engaged in military "crusades" against the Muslims, Francis, at great risk, walked through the lines, was captured and brought before the Sultan Melek el-Kamil and told the Muslim ruler about Jesus Christ. Speaking earlier this month in Harvard Chapel on the Feast Day of St. Francis, Dr. Bryan Hamlin said, "We know for certain that the Sultan was impressed and gave permission for Francis to visit the Holy places. Francis demonstrated a better way, the Christ-like way of dealing with your enemies, of reaching out to the difficult person."

My dictionary defines prayer both as a solemn request or thanksgiving to God or to an object of worship and the act of praying itself. Whether it is through request, thanksgiving or just the acknowledgement that there is a power outside ourselves, this day of prayer in Assisi will be significant.

There will be those who believe that, thanks to such prayer, God might choose to intervene in the world in some way to prevent war. And personally I do not see how you can believe that God can work a miracle in one individual among his four and a half billion souls and not also believe that he can have a global effect if he chooses to.

There will be those who will welcome the day as a chance to focus on what is important in our conduct of affairs, and those who welcome the chance to reflect on the life of St. Francis, and those who will regard the whole exercise as a waste of time.

Probably we will never know for sure what effect next Monday will have had on the world. But I would certainly agree with Tennyson who wrote, "More things are wrought by prayer than this world dreams of. Wherefore let thy voice rise like a fountain for me day and night."

By the way, St. Francis does just squeak into Seldes' book

of *The Great Thoughts* – as a passing negative reference in a quotation from Upton Sinclair.

October 23, 1986

A close shave

IN THE DARK brick confines of cell B24 the words of the old communion text came back to him and he started to sing, "In the same night as he was betrayed he took bread, and when he had given thanks he brake it. . . ." It was a long time since Leif had taken seriously anything to do with church.

Months before, when five Gestapo officers broke into his home in the early hours of the morning and bundled him into a car, he had been distinctly embarrassed when his mother called out, "Leif, don't forget Jesus." That sort of thing, he thought, was only for old women and invalids.

Leif Hovelsen was a teenager when he took part in the Norwegian Resistance movement. Betrayed by a friend, he found himself in solitary confinement awaiting execution. When I interviewed him in Portland on his current visit to the United States I had to repeat my questions several times because of the deafness caused by Gestapo beatings.

As the words of the communion came back to him, he told me, he suddenly realized what Jesus had gone through. "He had been betrayed and I had been betrayed. He had been tortured and I had been tortured. He had been crucified and I was going to be executed. It was as if Christ were physically walking beside me saying, 'Don't be afraid, Leif. I have been through all this for you. I am with you. I am the conqueror. Follow me.' "

Leif, at that point, felt that neither the Gestapo nor the

fear of execution had any longer any power over him. He was free. And he knelt down and prayed, "Whatever be your will, God, let that come to pass. But if I may live and even be free again, I give you the whole of my life to use as you see best."

This experience followed another profound moment two weeks earlier. Alone in his cell after a particularly brutal interrogation in which he had given more information than he wanted to, he knew he would not survive another session. Aware for the first time that he had been betrayed, realizing that his life and that of two of his friends depended on their telling the same story, the thought came, "Why not pray?"

He didn't believe in prayer. He argued with himself. But finally he decided to make the experiment. "God, if you exist," he prayed, "and you are here and see everything, then you know how helpless I am and what is at stake. Will you help Alvin and Erling to get through and say the right things." And he added, "If you can give me the answer and proof that you exist I will give myself wholly to you."

A few days later, Leif was suddenly taken out of his cell by the guard to get his hair cut. Which was strange, for it wasn't his turn. He was placed on a stool by the exit to the courtyard. For some reason the barber turned the stool to the left. Just then two other prisoners were marched down the stairs and halted opposite him while the two sets of guards conversed. It was Alvin and Erling. In the few seconds they had together they were able to establish that they had all told the same story.

Back in the cell Leif danced for joy, then suddenly remembered his prayer. Was it chance that he was taken out of turn to the barber, and that out of 450 prisoners those two should at that moment be transferred to another camp? Leif burst out, "God, I believe." Outside it was dark and dramatic, he recalls. There was thunder. "I was a different man."

Indeed, after the war he met another prisoner who, unknown to him, had been the one who shoved in his food tray each day and could observe him through the slot. "What happened to you?" he asked. "I was worried. You looked so depressed and down. Then one day you were so different. It was as if the whole cell was lit up. You had joy and peace of heart."

Another underpinning of what Leif calls his "lifetime walk with God" came a little later when he was moved from the Gestapo cells to a concentration camp. He had got to know a Christian prisoner, Olaf, and they had shared their hopes and longings. Then one day Olaf was condemned to death and taken to another cell. Before the evening roll call Leif walked under the cell's window. "I so wanted to show solidarity." Other prisoners were milling around, including some radical intellectuals he was eager to please.

Suddenly Olaf pulled himself up by the bars, his eyes took them all in and in a strong, clear voice he called out, "Thanks for your comradeship, Leif. Never give up in the fight for Christ." Leif looked at his other friends and said nothing. When roll call was over he went back to his room to be alone. He thought about Peter when he heard the cock crow, and he wept. "It was like Christ touching me and saying, 'Don't be distressed, stand up and follow me,' " Leif says. "I decided never again to deny the truth of Christ and to follow him regardless of my shortcomings."

Today, because of his wartime experiences, Leif is a trusted ally of many East European dissidents who feel that he shares with them an awareness of what it is like to lose freedom. He is a member of the Norwegian Helsinki Watch Committee. He is also a friend of many Germans because soon after the war he forgave the man who tortured him, even refusing to press charges, and stretched out a hand of friendship to his former oppressors.

"It all goes back," he says, "to my Easter experience in the camp. God gave me life. It was for a purpose. I'm never bogged down with bitterness or bad feelings about people, It's a wonderful gift."

April 16, 1987

If the cap fits . . .

IF ONLY the leaders would get out of the way we ordinary people would solve our differences.
How often you hear variations on that theme.
I heard it again at a meeting this past week, and everyone present responded with the usual sympathetic murmurs. It touches on a longing in all of us for better leadership, and easy answers, and a less threatening world.
Personally, however, I find the thought irritatingly naive as well as hopelessly impractical, and even a trifle arrogant. It represents an exaggerated view of leaders' vices and an inflated view of our own virtues.
As Walter Lippman wrote fifty years ago, "We must adopt the habit of thinking as plainly about the sovereign people as we do about the politicians they elect. It will not do to think poorly about the politicians, and to talk with bated breath about the voters. No more than kings before them should the people be hedged with divinity. Like all princes and rulers, like all sovereigns, they are ill-served by flattery and adulation."
I am actually grateful that our leaders know a lot more than I do and am skeptical that I would necessarily do any better than they do. I have met enough leaders to know that many are not the scheming men and women who have sold their souls that some make them out to be, and I have met enough self-centered people who are not leaders to be skeptical of them as replacements.
Of course, the remark "if only leaders would get out of the way" is really just one of those things we say, that we take comfort from and which means nothing. There will always be leaders. The fact that we go on saying it, however, does indicate that we sometimes like to indulge in wishful thinking or perhaps to talk without thought at all.
The truth is that we all, leaders and led, are cut from the same cloth and need to find a new way of doing things. In our democratic societies we get on the whole the leaders we deserve. So if we want new leadership we may have to start

with new qualities in those from whose ranks the leaders are drawn.

For starters, we will have to decide that we want to change, not follow, public opinion. We will have to dethrone the great God Gallup and all the pollsters he has spawned. And, if the Danish theologian Soren Kierkegaard is to be believed, that will be an uphill task. He wrote, "The truth must essentially be regarded as in conflict with this world; the world has never been so good, and will never become so good that the majority will desire the truth."

We may have to reestablish public service as the motive for seeking public office, rather than seeing appointments as the chance to advance a personal agenda, as a stepping stone, perhaps, to public relations and the private sector, even to big bucks and bestsellerhood.

Columnist Georgie Anne Geyer describes the story of our times as: "Greedy American politician desiring to be instant celebrity hooks up by historic accident with American adversarial journalist." She writes, "These two illogical allies were orphans left behind when the Puritan ethic died slowly about a decade ago. Celebrityism took over from the concept of honorable service to people and nation. Public life became public theater."

We may have to clarify what is and what is not acceptable behavior. I read in an editorial in *The Oregonian* this week, "Resignation on principle is not a general practice in American politics." That's no doubt true. But it is probably also true, as David Ignatius wrote earlier this year in the *Washington Post*, "There was a time when it was typical for officials who disagreed with administration policy, or who felt their useful service had come to an end, to do the proper thing and resign." Should we not work to restore that standard.

We may also need to reenthrone the concept of right and wrong, a notion which, as Meg Greenfield wrote in *Newsweek*, "has become politically and personally embarrassing." She suggests that right and wrong have been replaced by right and stupid, right and not necessarily constitutional, right and sick, right and only to be expected, and right and complex. She says, "As I listen to the moral arguments swirling about this summer I become even more persuaded that our real problem is this: the 'still, small voice' of conscience has become far too small – and utterly still."

A much respected Australian political figure, Kim Beazley, Sr., echoes that thought. "If you do not accept the importance of conscience, you accept only the importance of power," he writes.

A recent nationwide poll found that a third of young adults feel that it is sometimes justified to steal from their employer. Employee theft adds up to 15% to the price of consumer goods. Cheating on income taxes costs the federal government $100 billion each year. That's not leaders. That's us. And that is where the new leadership may have to begin. Whenever we cut corners morally we undercut our ability to challenge our leaders to higher moral standards.

Congressman Lee Hamilton says rightly, "Americans are fed up with politicians and leaders telling them how to live, but are themselves living less than exemplary lives." I suspect that politicians may also sometimes, though they would never say it, get fed up with constituents who demand a higher standard from them than they would accept themselves.

Perhaps, on second thought, *we* should take the place of our leaders. But I wonder how long it would be before there was an outcry for us to be replaced.

A more lasting solution may be for us to learn together.

October 16, 1986